PUBLIC

SPEAKING

Build Charismatic Self-esteem & Learn the Science
to Talk to Anyone With Effective Social and
Emotional Intelligence & Conversation Skills

(Gain Confidence and Feel Free From Anxiety)

Garr Gallo

Published by Rob Miles

Public Speaking: Build Charismatic Self-esteem & Learn the Science to Talk to Anyone With Effective Social and Emotional Intelligence & Conversation Skills (Gain Confidence and Feel Free From Anxiety)

ISBN 978-1-989990-07-0

Legal & Disclaimer

The information contained in this book is not designed to replace or take the place of any form of medicine or professional medical advice. The information in this book has been provided for educational and entertainment purposes only.

The information contained in this book has been compiled from sources deemed reliable, and it is accurate to the best of the Author's knowledge; however, the Author cannot guarantee its accuracy and validity and cannot be held liable for any errors or omissions. Changes are periodically made to this book. You must consult your doctor or get professional medical advice before using any of the suggested remedies, techniques, or information in this book.

Table of Contents

Introduction

However, that is not what this book is designed to help you do. This book is designed to help you, as an entrepreneur, increase what I like to call "coins and contacts." If you are an entrepreneur and you sell products or services, then every time you open your mouth to talk about your business you should be collecting coins and/or contacts. EVERYTIME! Yes indeed.

My goal is that by the time you finish reading this book, you will be able to identify how you can succeed at speaking in public, and know how to collect these "coins and contacts."

Keep in mind that when you are done reading this, you will understand how to develop your talk regardless of whether it is for a networking event or for an event where you are a highlighted speaker. You are going to learn the tools you need as a speaker, including how to get booked as a speaker, how to get over the number one reason why most people never develop their public speaking skills, and more!

Trust me, this book is going to be a great addition to your personal development library. I will also say that once you are done with this book, make sure to visit the sites that I reference so that you can take your reading to another level!

Again, congratulations on making the right choice. I know without a doubt that the person who can effectively communicate to others is also the person who makes the most money! To your journey and to your success!

Chapter 1: Character Development

Your public speaking journey does not begin the moment you stand on stage to deliver a speech. Nor does it begin when you start writing and practicing a speech. It begins when you make a decision to start working on your inner self.

Many think that learning public speaking is all about mastering voice projection, hand gestures and body movement. However, in focusing on delivery techniques only, you may fall into the trap of using these techniques as ends of themselves and not as means to deliver your message. The thing to remember is: public speaking techniques cannot outgrow who you are.

If your hand gestures are not stemming from an inner drive you can come across as affected. If you move on the stage but there is no motivation to connect with the audience it can come across as mechanical. If you display a smile and have open and precise body language without being confident on the inside it can be misinterpreted as fake.

Drawing on the analogy of a car, compare your inner self to an engine and public speaking techniques to a car's body. It is best practice to match the engine's capacity with the body's size. A car manufacturer does not put a small engine in a truck or a truck's engine in a small car. Similarly, in public speaking, to be a truly authentic speaker, you have to match delivery techniques with how you feel on the inside. You don't want to use grand gestures when you are not passionate about the speech content and you don't want to limit yourselves to standing still when you just want to jump for joy about a topic.

The character development stage considers the following:

First is **how to develop the mindset of a public speaker**. Having a positive mindset is essential to succeed in any area of life. It is the foundation that our attitudes, behaviours and actions rest upon. It's very important to develop the right mindset about public speaking before you attempt to learn anything else about it.

Second is **how to overcome fear**. Fear of public speaking is so powerful that it can override the entire learning process. For many, when they say "I want to learn public speaking" what they actually mean is "I want to learn how to overcome my fear of public speaking". In order to deliver dynamic speeches and connect effectively with the audience you need to be willing to expose your vulnerabilities, be honest with yourself and cope with others having an opinion about you. You cannot do any of this without overcoming fear.

Third is **how to speak from the heart.** The secret to becoming an engaging public speaker is to speak from the heart. In the absence of this, your words, gestures and body language can cause you come across as dry, mechanical and fake. When you speak from the heart it doesn't matter whether the topic is exciting or mundane, you can always find an approach to convey genuine passion about it.

Character development is the first stage in learning public speaking. Once you work on your inner self you would able to learn and naturally apply all techniques of public speaking. Your confidence and passion will shine and help you build a connection with the audience far beyond what words and gestures can do alone.

SECTION 1

HOW TO DEVELOP THE MINDSET OF A PUBLIC SPEAKER

"The mind is everything, what you think

you become"

~ Buddha

Having a positive mindset is essential to succeed in any area of life. It is the foundation that our attitudes, behaviours and actions are built upon. It's very important to develop a healthy mindset about public speaking before attempting to learn anything else about it. Below are six core beliefs about public speaking that will help in your public speaking journey.

1. OVERCOMING FEAR OF PUBLIC SPEAKING IS NOT THE SAME AS LEARNING PUBLIC SPEAKING

When many people say 'I want to learn public speaking' what they actually mean is: 'I want to learn how to overcome my fear of public speaking'. Fear of public speaking is so powerful that it can override the entire learning process. People often learn speaking techniques not because they want to deliver an engaging speech but because they want to feel safe by hiding behind rules. They say to themselves - 'I am following public speaking best practice therefore no-one can criticise me'. While this approach may give some temporary relief from fear, it does not deal with the root cause. This is counter-productive for a number of reasons.

Firstly, it generates a false confidence based on external measures and means instead of real confidence that stems from within. If you don't deal with fear from its root you will be afraid whenever you deliver a speech.

Secondly, it uses public speaking techniques for the wrong purpose. In public speaking there are techniques to overcome fear, techniques to connect with the audience, techniques to deliver an easy to follow massage, the list goes on. When the motivation is only to overcome fear, you end up using all these techniques motivated completely by fear. By doing so, the real purpose of each technique is lost. This increases the risk of being unable to connect with the audience and coming across as mechanical.

2. NERVOUSNESS AND FEAR ARE NOT THE SAME THING – NERVOUSNESS IS HELPFUL

Nervousness is the energy you feel before delivering a speech. It's the energy of excitement, anticipation and of being the centre of attention. Fear is what you feel when you perceive this energy in a negative way. When you deliver a speech you want to be nervous to a certain extent. Nervousness shows that you care about the topic and have a connection to it. Nerves will energise you and cause you to shine on stage. Without nerves you run the risk of coming across as flat and consequently less able to captivate the audience.

Nervousness is an energy. Perceive it in a negative way and it will hinder you. Perceive it in a positive way and it will empower you.

3. PUBLIC SPEAKING IS ABOUT SHARING A MESSAGE

It is not about pleasing the boss, tricking the crowd into thinking that you are confident or getting the speech out of the way. The purpose of any speech is sharing a message with the audience. The message is defined as what you are talking about and why you are talking about it. Everything else should align with this. Unfortunately a lot of speakers are not aware of this. When they are asked to deliver a speech they feel nervous and they start thinking of ways to ease their nervousness. They set goals like trying to please the boss, trying to come across confident or just to get the speech out of the way as fast as possible. The problem is these goals don't work simply because public speaking is not meant to achieve them. Public speaking is about sharing your message with the audience in an effective way. Focus on this and everything else will fall into place much more easily.

4. PUBLIC SPEAKING IS ABOUT SHARING BOTH THOUGHTS AND EMOTIONS

Public speaking is not about delivering information only. Emails and articles can achieve this and in many cases more effectively. Public speaking is about reaching the audience on an emotional level, to make them feel what you feel, understand the importance or urgency of something, share your passion or just to make them feel good. Think about it - why do we still deliver speeches and presentations in today's world when we can deliver the same information to millions of people with one click of a button? It's because, unlike articles or emails, public speaking allows us to communicate on an emotional level. For example, imagine you want to say via email that something is important. You might highlight the piece of information in red, write "important" in the email subject or tag the email with a exclamation mark. Recipients will know on a logical level that this information is important but probably they won't feel how you feel about it. Now imagine you ran over to the same group of people in the office and everything about you showed how important the information was - your voice, body language, facial expressions and the pace of your speech. Most probably they would feel the importance of what you are going to say even before you say a single word. Which scenario do you think will get a more immediate response? Public speaking can reach people on an emotional level and achieve a response much more effectively than any other mass communication medium can achieve.

5. PUBLIC SPEAKING IS ABOUT BRINGING THE REAL YOU ON STAGE

The most engaging public speakers are the ones who come across natural on stage. They are not the ones with the most elaborate hand gestures or the ones with the most precise body language. Unfortunately however, when many people think about learning public speaking they think about only learning techniques such as voice projection, hand gestures and body movement. Whilst this is a very important part of it, it is not the whole story. To be an engaging, authentic public speaker it is important that you use these techniques without losing the real you on stage.

6. NO ONE IS BORN A NATURAL SPEAKER. SPEECHES REQUIRE A LOT OF PRACTICE AND PREPARATION

It's interesting how when we see highly skilled athletes or artists we automatically assume that they have put countless hours of preparation and practice into achieving their skills. Yet when it comes to highly skilled public speakers we tend to assume that they were simply born that way. One reason we do so is because unlike other activities, speaking is something we have been doing ever since we learned how to speak. We subconsciously believe that we have reached our speaking potential already and think that we cannot improve anymore. The truth is, public speaking is a skill just like any other. It requires extensive preparation and practice. No one is born a natural speaker. Just because we walk everyday doesn't mean we can naturally walk on a tightrope. The same goes for public speaking.

SECTION 2

HOW TO OVERCOME THE FEAR OF PUBLIC SPEAKING

"There are two types of speakers: those who are nervous

and those who are liars!"

~ Mark Twain

For many people when they say 'I want to learn public speaking' what they actually mean is 'I want to learn how to overcome my fear of public speaking'. Fear of public speaking is so powerful that it can override the entire learning process. Below are seven ways to help you overcome this fear.

1. REALISE THAT YOU ARE NOT ALONE

A major source of the fear of public speaking is feeling like you are the only one with that fear. Public speaking is one of the most common fears in the world. Studies suggest that this fear is often greater than the fear of death itself. Even those with a career that revolves around speaking are often still very afraid of it. Radio presenters, lecturers and even actors can all fall victim to this fear. Some people are so overwhelmed by the fear that they take it to the extreme by quitting their jobs to avoid it. Fear of public speaking is a natural human reaction that many people share. Knowing your are not alone can be comforting as you overcome your own fear (but it is not an excuse to stay afraid, you can overcome it!).

2. UNDERSTAND YOU ARE YOUR OWN WORST CRITIC

A major source of the fear of public speaking is fear of criticism. You imagine that the audience are holding a microscope over your insecurities, judging you, and just waiting for you to fail. The truth is, each of us tends to be his or her own worst critic. The audience don't see what you see – The memory lapse accompanied by a pause that you felt lasted for a lifetime was probably no more than a second long. The stutter and stumble over a phrase that you thought people would make fun of, probably went unnoticed. The audience is far less critical than you may think. Be less harsh on yourself and you will overcome any fear of criticism which in turn will set you free from the fear of public speaking.

3. BE VERY CLEAR ABOUT YOUR MESSAGE

A major source of the fear of public speaking is the fear of being misunderstood. Being misunderstood can make you feel lonely, disappointed and even depressed. No wonder many fear it and try their best to avoid it. The best way to overcome being misunderstood is to be very clear about the message. You can achieve that by making sure in each speech you answer one of the following three questions: How? Why? or What? For example, suppose you were asked to deliver a presentation about climate change. Without having clear direction you can become overwhelmed by such a broad topic and ultimately be misunderstood by the audience. However, you can narrow the topic down by making it answer one of the three questions as follows:

- How can we overcome climate change?

- Why do we need to overcome climate change?

- What can we do to overcome climate change?

Once you are very clear about the message, you can overcome a major source of fear of public speaking - fear of being misunderstood.

4. MASTER YOUR FEAR OF FAILURE

A major source of the fear of public speaking is the fear of failure. Failure can make you feel inadequate, it can magnify any shortcomings and it can shake your confidence.

There are many ways to address the fear of failure. Firstly, it is important to realise that most things feared don't actually happen in reality. The audience won't laugh at you, you won't faint, nor forget chunks of the speech.

Secondly, it is important to remember that failure is inevitable on the path to success. For instance, the cliche example, how many times did you fall when learning how to walk? Hundreds of times! Instead of fearing failure, embrace it. Failure signifies you have tried and are a step closer to success.

Thirdly, don't allow failure to define who you are. No one is born an expert. As Niels Bohr said: "An expert is a person who has made all the mistakes that can be made in a very narrow field." Think of failure as a step towards becoming who you are meant to be. Failure only defines who you are when you allow it to prevent you from dusting yourself off and trying again.

5. REMEMBER THE AUDIENCE IS A COLLECTION OF INDIVIDUALS WITH DIFFERENT BELIEFS AND ATTITUDES

Another major source of fear of public speaking is the belief that the audience is one group, with one belief and one attitude. Many speakers feel that the audience is like an army that would charge at them should they say what it doesn't want to hear. The reality is, the audience is a collection of individuals with different beliefs and attitudes. An audience member on one side of the room may totally disagree with a member on the other side. The only thing that the audience has in common is that they are listening to you. Keeping this thought in mind next time you deliver a speech will give you a lot of confidence.

6. VISUALISE DELIVERING A SPEECH

There is no doubt the best way to overcome fear of public speaking is to deliver speeches regularly. However, it can be challenging to get speaking opportunities and hence you don't always get enough practice.

Visualising yourself delivering a speech is one way to tackle this. It allows you to live the experience in your mind. When you master the art of visualisation, you can literally experience the physical symptoms of fear – increased heart rate, sweaty palms and even dry mouth.

To visualise delivering a speech effectively start by imagining yourself standing in front of an audience. Try to visualise the room, the number of people, the time of the day and the facial expressions of the audience. The more details you can imagine the more realistic your experience will be. If it is challenging to visualise an audience, one option is to view images of audiences online and imagine yourself delivering a speech to them. Another way is to walk along a busy street and imagine talking to the people you encounter.

Once the experience begins to feel real, try to trace your emotions. How do you feel? Why do you feel that way? Can you handle the emotion or do you find it overwhelming? If you can handle it, increase the size of the audience in your mind. If you find it overwhelming take a step back and try to understand why it makes you afraid. Harnessing the power of visualisation is very useful when practicing any speech.

7. DELIVER AS MANY SPEECHES AS POSSIBLE

Delivering speeches regularly is one of the most effective ways to overcome the fear of public speaking. The more speeches you deliver the more comfortable you will become. Overcoming the fear of public speaking is like learning to ride a bicycle. You can't do it by reading, thinking and visualisation alone. You have to get on the bike and go for a ride as many times as possible. Whilst you may fall and feel pain initially, once you find your balance it starts to come naturally. The same goes for public speaking.

SECTION 3

HOW TO SPEAK FROM THE HEART

"You can speak well if your tongue can deliver

 the message of your heart"

~ John Ford

The secret to becoming an engaging public speaker is to speak from the heart. Without it your words, gestures and body language can come across dry, mechanical and fake. When you speak from the heart it doesn't matter whether the topic is exciting or mundane, you can always find an approach to convey genuine passion about it. Here are six ways to learn how to speak from your heart.

1. UNDERSTAND WHAT SPEAKING FROM THE HEART IS

Speaking from the heart is speaking with emotions. It does not necessarily mean speaking with sadness. It can be any emotions - joy, a sense of urgency, hope.

To demonstrate what is meant by speaking from the heart consider joke telling. Sometimes you hear the same joke, word for word, from two different people and the outcome is completely different. From one person it is funny and makes you laugh, from the other it barely makes you crack a smile! How can the same joke have such different results? On a logical level it doesn't make sense – the joke is exactly the same! The difference lies on an emotional level. The funny person did not just say the joke, they felt the joke so others could feel it too. The other joke teller that failed did not feel it so neither did others.

When you genuinely feel what you are saying the audience will feel it too. This in essence of speaking from the heart.

2. REALISE THE IMPORTANCE OF SPEAKING FROM THE HEART

Speaking from the heart is the secret ingredient for any speaker. It has many benefits including:

Firstly, it connects you with the audience. When you speak from the heart you connect with the audience in a way that is far beyond words.

Secondly, it helps you overcome any fears associated with public speaking and it makes you a more natural speaker.

Thirdly, it helps you understand the purpose of public speaking techniques and you start applying them intuitively.

Finally, it can give you that x-factor - the most sought after trait in public speaking!

3. MAKE SURE YOU BELIEVE IN YOUR MESSAGE

To speak from the heart it is vital that you believe in your message. When you believe in your message everything about the speech becomes easier. Your belief acts like an engine that will drive you during writing, practicing and delivery. It will fuel your confidence, enable you to naturally connect with the audience and you will enjoy delivering the speech.

To check whether you believe in your message ask yourself: How do I feel about it? Do I really care? Am I excited? Do I want others to know about it? If the answer is no then try to tweak or change the message until you find something you truly believe in.

4. MAKE SURE YOUR INTERNAL AND EXTERNAL MOTIVATIONS ARE IN HARMONY

As a speaker you are guaranteed to come across as fake if your internal and external motivations are not in harmony. For example, a speaker may tell a joke because he wants the audience to think he is funny and not because he genuinely wants the audience to laugh. Similarly when a speaker shares an inspirational story because they want to sell more books rather than to inspire the audience, the internal and external motivations are not in harmony.

The audience, whether consciously or unconsciously can sense a speaker's internal motivations. If they don't match the external motivations the audience has a tendency to lose interest and feel an emotional barrier between themselves and the speaker. The result is the audience will not think the speaker is funny or be motivated to buy the book. In other words, the audience simply won't buy into any of it.

5. WHEN REHEARSING, PRACTICE YOUR EMOTIONS TOO

When many people practice their speeches they tend to practice saying words and delivery techniques only. As a speaker, you need to recognise the importance of practicing the emotions behind your words as well.

Say for example you wanted to communicate that a charity you are involved with raised $10,000 last month. If your charity usually raises $7,000 a month then this is exciting news. If it usually raises $15,000 then the news is disappointing. The same sentence could be exciting or disappointing depending on the context. If you practice the words only you won't be able to convey your ideas and thoughts as effectively.

When practicing think of how you feel about the words you are saying. Try to live the emotion while saying the words out loud. The emotion will be reflected in your tone of voice, body language and in your facial expressions. It is important to note that you must avoid trying to manufacture emotions. That is, forcing yourself to feel something you are not. This will make you come across as fake. If you feel the emotion in your words while practicing this will translate in your actual delivery.

6. WHEN DELIVERING, FOCUS ON YOUR MESSAGE AND YOUR MESSAGE ONLY

You have memorised your speech, practiced, learned all the techniques about public speaking (later in the book) and now it is time to deliver your speech. The most important thing to keep in mind is that when delivering your speech you don't want to think about anything except your message. You don't want to worry about forgetting your lines, not using an open body language, umming and arring, not moving on stage, etc. These are things to worry about during practicing and not during delivery. When you deliver your speech focus on your message and your message only. This will free you from any stress and allows to connect with the audience on a deeper level.

Chapter 2: Pulling Down The Curtains On Anxiety

When you prepare for a presentation or a speech there will always be a bit of anxiety. This just cannot be helped. We have this built-in mechanism that signals anxiety automatically when we face certain situations, and in this case, public speaking. There's no perfect presentation. On the other hand, when we make a presentation and then realize we made some mistakes, our brain then automatically focuses more on the mistakes rather than the entirety of the speech. This simply confirms such fears and builds up anxiety even more. However, anxiety can be overcome but first you must understand how it happens and how to control it.

What Triggers the Fear of Public Speaking?

Anxiety brought upon by public speaking is basically the fear of embarrassment or being judged. This is because of all the attention that is centered on the speaker at the moment of the presentation. In each presentation, the ideal thing to do would be to speak clearly and loudly. However, the feeling of self-doubt is always present especially with all the attention given to each word you speak. Aside from self-doubt, the fear of embarrassment, or being judged, there are also other causes for public speaking anxiety.

A lot of individuals nowadays are more inclined to stay online somewhere in an enclosed location like their homes. This lack of public interaction causes these individuals to feel discomfort with public speaking and lessens their chances of ever engaging in one.

In this digital age, work becomes less interactive in a physical way. People are using phones, e-mails, and chat applications to convey information. The physical interaction between human to human is starting to disappear as today, the interaction is becoming more of man-machine-man. Although this isn't an alarming thing but future public speakers would find it harder as relative experience is lacking.

It actually doesn't really matter whether or not you're a seasoned public speaker or a younger one. The thing is, modern day life is making interaction with other people seemingly lesser than it was before. However, this only accounts for a small portion of anxiety. There are other causes for anxiety which may have deeper roots and may require different tactics to go about and cure anxiety.

How to Calm your Nerves and Reduce Anxiety

It is common to encounter even the least bit of anxiety as you ready yourself for an upcoming presentation or speech. Even some of the most experienced speakers in the world get a little bit anxious when they are about to hit the stage in front of a really huge crowd. You must not ever expect yourself to be completely free of anxiety. Instead, you must use the anxiety to perform well enough to deliver a great presentation and not the other way around.

In scenarios where public speaking gets the best out of you, it might be time to get yourself some help. The main concern is our tendency to focus all of our attention on the mistakes we make which in turn, makes it hard for us to get over anxiety immediately. It just takes that single mistake to fuel our fears but it's so hard to extinguish that flame.

To be able to break free from your public speaking anxiety, you must make smart decisions prior to speaking, during, and after your presentation. Some individuals get scared and anxious when publicly speaking in front of their friends whom are mixed in a large crowd. That type of anxiety is more of social phobia which may require a different course of action.

Things to do Before Making a Speech

In this instance, what you need to learn is to control or cure public speaking anxiety. It mainly requires a well-though plan and the choice of executing them. Here they are

Prior to your Speech

Practice, and Practice some more!

Relax and visualize yourself.

Don't reject embarrassment, instead, accept it!

During the day of the speech

Complete muscle relaxation

Meditate

After the speech

Write down positive remarks instead of mistakes

Repeat cycle but this time with lesser anxiety and more preparation

Basically, public speaking anxiety grows bigger as the big date draws nearer. However, there are methods on how you could control anxiety and turn from something destructive into something constructive. First and foremost, practice is extremely essential. Rehearse your lines so you won't forget them. Don't be overconfident thinking that you already know what to say. You'll only become more anxious the moment you forget your lines. It's always a good thing to be confident but taking it to a higher level usually does more harm than good.

Try to think about yourself on that stage giving out your presentation. Think of how you're going to deliver your speech on stage. Visualize yourself thinking of every possible scenario. Take into account everything. Think about how you could perfectly give out your speech and imagine some with a few mistakes and from there come up with a backup plan on how you could easily recover.

Instead of feeling embarrassed, treat your mistakes as your next target. Think of them as the key points that you need to improve. And just bear in mind, nobody's perfect. So, if someone

Chapter 3: Getting It On

Iwas pleased to learn that my coach would be Martin. I knew he'd be honest with his feedback. He'd tell me what works and what doesn't. We all need to know what we're doing well because sometimes we get obsessed with our own faults. That said, we do need to know what's not working. As another trainer I work with puts it: "It's the poppy seed effect. If you're at a cocktail party and you eat one of those canapés with black seeds on top, then have a poppy seed stuck in your teeth, you'd rather someone told you than smile at everyone all evening with it."

Martin and I got together several times to flesh out my idea of "piercing the pomposity of people who take themselves too seriously". By now, we had realised that this topic couldn't be tackled adequately in a three-minute "palate cleanser" spot, and Jane and Harrison agreed to upgrade me to a full speaking slot. The TED guidelines state that 18 minutes is the maximum length for a standard talk, but in recent years they've discovered that less is more in terms of online views. I was allocated 11 minutes by TEDxBasel.

I had already been through several drafts of the speech by the date all speakers had been instructed to submit their scripts. The speeches would then be vetted and edited by the two people at the head of TEDxBasel, something I'd not expected from an organisation affiliated with TED, which is devoted to "spreading ideas". You don't imagine anyone taking a red pen to Al Gore.

By this time, I had already decided to put aside my pre-conceived ideas as a communication and presentation trainer myself. This time, I would take on the TED experience from the inside, as a speaker. I reckoned that immersing myself in the process the TEDxBasel organisers were about to put me through would be a learning experience for me as a speaker, as well as a trainer afterwards.

I was on my way to a friend's Eurovision night when I had an appointment at Jane and Harrison's apartment in the trendiest area of Basel to go through the latest version of the script and decide on the final direction of the talk. They gave me some feedback and the three of us came up with some further ways of developing the talk. Overall they were pleased with how it was progressing.

After a couple more sessions with Martin, my script was shaping up well. I had dropped one of the initial concepts that seemed to be constricting the shape of the talk, as well as one or two anecdotes that were taking up time but not adding to the idea. Here's one:

My ten-year-old daughter is a fabulous literal thinker. I once asked her "Patti, if frankfurters are from Frankfurt, and hamburgers are from Hamburg, where is Wiener Schnitzel from?" She thought for a moment and then said "Venus?"

Every sentence matters when you have a limited time to talk, and even though a tale like that might get an audience to smile, you need to be ruthless with your words.

I've mentioned the importance of getting feedback so that you can uncover blind spots and amplify strong points. I'd decided that my talk was now in such an advanced stage as to be tested on a virgin audience, one who had not yet been exposed to my speech at all.

I'd been running a series of presentation training courses alongside an expert speaker trainer, Olivia Schofield. With the permission of her training group, I performed my talk in front of them. I say "performed" but it was more like "read out aloud".

You see, according to the strict TED process Jane and Harrison had instructed us to follow, we were required to recite the entire script word for word. Parrot-fashion is something I have never asked the people I've trained to do. I've always found that speakers who aren't trained actors can get hung up on memorising scripts. Memorised speeches can often lack freshness, authenticity, and a sense of spontaneity. But I'd agreed to go along with the TEDxBasel process and adhere to it, so I would.

My audience gave me some valuable points of feedback. Olivia then reviewed my script and did something that transformed my ramblings into sharpened prose: she took a red pen and ruthlessly struck out every unnecessary word or phrase. It gave the words space and drama.

Here's an example, from my opening lines:

Before...

I was at BBC Television Centre in London. They used to call it the concrete doughnut. A big, grey sixties building that dominated Shepherd's Bush. The studio lights were about to go up on a prestigious TV debate show. I had always wanted to be on the telly, ever since I was a child. I was in my suit and tie feeling really important, sweating with nerves and anxiety, sitting... in the audience, watching.

After...

BBC Television Centre, London. The studio lights dimmed on a prestigious TV debate show. I was in my suit and tie feeling really important, sweating with nerves and anxiety, sitting... in the audience.

Now my speech was really getting into shape. It was shorter, sharper, and stronger. I'd been lucky enough to have had feedback from some of the world's finest presentation trainers: Olivia had passed it to a couple of trainers she works with and they had provided some excellent guidance.

Chapter 4: How To Use Your Voice

Your voice is a powerful weapon during any presentation. The classic advice is that by hitting the right intonation, you can draw your audience into the speech and captivate them with your words.

Blah, blah, blah.

That shouldn't be your goal here. Instead, your goal should be to avoid the common verbal mistakes people make when speaking.

Often, public speaking coaches focus on having their students talk excitedly or put emphasis on key words to highlight something. This advice is entirely wrong.

Here's why: a bad verbal presentation with emphasis on key words is still a lousy presentation. A good verbal presentation without emphasis on key words is still a good presentation.

So rather than looking at how we can put emphasis on words, we're going to talk about eliminating the three verbal issues we all have in presentations. If you eliminate each one of these three, your verbal will almost always be good in a presentation.

Filler Words

Filler words are widespread. We all use them in some capacity, but they have a nasty habit of appearing more within presentations. These are words such as: "umm," "ahh," and "like." They appear much more frequently than we realize because we don't hear ourselves saying them. As a society, we say "like" so much that we don't even notice it anymore.

That is until an audience is listening to you present. Then, you can be sure they hear you saying "like!"

The goal here is to teach yourself not to use filler words. The general advice here is to videotape yourself, then watch back to realize how many times you use the word "like." That is not a helpful exercise, and you're better off ignoring it.

The reason why is watching the videotape provides no new information. All the video shows you is that you use filler words. That's not helpful, because we all use filler words. You already knew that already. Even worse, it's after-the-fact, so you can't adjust mid-presentation.

Filler Word Exercise: Raise your hand

Instead, find a partner to practice your presentation with. Give your presentation to your partner. Your partner will sit and listen to your speech. Every time your partner hears a filler word, they will raise their hand.

As the presenter, you'll be shocked at the number of times they will raise their hand. However, you are getting live feedback about the number of times you use filler words. It will help you start to course correct and remove filler words from your presentation vocabulary during your practice.

In the past, students of mine have been able to altogether remove filler words by doing this exercise just a few times. Give it a short-I promise it will work for you!

Speaking too quickly

Another common verbal presentation issue. I've found that many speakers will rush through their words, typically due to nerves. However, there is a bit of a growing trend where we tend to idolize those we speak quickly. Society is beginning to view speaking quickly as a sign of intelligence or excitement.

However, that leads to more mistakes when presenting than anything else. Many speakers lose their train of thought. Even worse, the audience typically cannot follow the presentation. Remember, your goal in presenting is to communicate your message. If you speak too quickly, your audience will lose track of what your message is.

Speaking too quickly exercise: five-second pause

This exercise can be done without a partner. We're going to force ourselves to over-correct here. Begin practicing your presentation to yourself. Pull out your phone or use an online stopwatch.

At the end of every single sentence, start the stopwatch. You need to wait five seconds before you can begin the next sentence. After five seconds, start the next sentence. Then, pause again.

Repeat this process until you have gone through your entire speech. As you can guess, it will probably take a while and feel extremely unnatural.

Then, give your presentation again. This time, without a stopwatch. I guarantee you'll present at an appropriate, slower pace!

Intonation

This is a significant issue. Intonation is when your words slowly get LOUDER AS A SENTENCE GETS LONGER. It tends to pop up when PEOPLE GET MORE AND MORE NERVOUS.

In my opinion, this is the worst of the three verbal issues. The reason why is it's the most distracting to your audience. That means it's also the most distracting from your message you want to communicate. Once your audience hears your intonation, it's hard for them to hear anything else.

Intonation exercise: Whisper

Unfortunately, intonation is also the hardest to solve. I had intonation myself for a while, which is not something you hear an award-winning public speaking coach admit that often!

To fix intonation, you need a partner again. The reason is that we often don't realize that we are getting louder as the sentence progresses. In fact, it's harder for us to realize we are using intonation that it is for us realize we are using filler words.

That's where the partner comes in! Again, give your practice presentation to your partner. Any time they think you are getting louder as the sentence progresses, they will raise their hand.

As the speaker, your job is to then get quieter on the next sentence. As you go through the sentence, speak softer until the last word of the sentence needs is said so quietly that it is basically a whisper.

Then, return to average volume on the next sentence.

Keep doing this exercise until your partner no longer raises their hand. It could take a couple times doing this exercise, spread out across a couple days.

However, this exercise will teach you to recognize when you are using intonation. Even better, it will teach you how to fix intonation.

Chapter 5: Why Is It Difficult To Get Rid Of Public

speaking fear?

Many of us are aware of this study which indicates that -the biggest fear in this world is the fear of public speaking.

keep this fear aside for a moment. Let's talk about some other fears. Imagine for a moment that you have fear of water. To get rid of the fear of water you have to face the water, you have to get into the water, of course, you will take someone's help but the only way to get rid of the fear of water is-face water.

Imagine for a moment you have fear of heights. How you will get rid of this fear? Of course, you will go on heights under some supervision. But the only way to get rid of the fear of height is-face height.

Similarly, if you have fear of public speaking the only way to get rid of the fear of public speaking is to face the public, stand in front of the public. But where is the public? The public (people)is busy. Sometimes it's very difficult to ask four to five people to sit in front of you so that you can deliver your talk. They all are busy in their lives.

The biggest problem with the fear of public speaking is that

even if you decide to get rid of the fear of public speaking public is not available. The way water is available. Heights are available. The public is not available.

That's the reason for years' people fail to manage to get rid of the fear of public speaking.

So my suggestion to you is- create opportunities in your life so that you can stand and speak in front of the public. It could be as simple as this-Imagine for a moment that you are sitting in a conference as an audience and when

the speaker asks "any question?" you should be the first person to raise the hand. You're asking a question and at the same time you are facing the public so you can get rid of public speaking fear. Do this every time. Of course no need to say that you should have a question.

In your office, in your home, create opportunities to stand alone and speak. Join some public speaking clubs like Toastmasters. Go to open mics where you can stand and speak, doesn't matter even if it is a small group, facing the public will help you to get rid of the fear of public speaking.

I feel nervous on the stage

we have seen so many people who don't go on the stage just because they feel nervous.

They believe that if they go on the stage, they will look nervous they will feel nervousness. You know what, if you are feeling nervous on the stage it means only one thing you are a human being. Yes, only humans feel nervous. Robots and machines don't feel nervous.

Even according to Mark Twain the legend, he says "There are only two types of speakers nervous speakers and Liars" Feeling nervous on the stage is absolutely natural. Of course, there are techniques for looking confident on the stage, there are techniques for concealing your nervousness, hiding your nervousness, masking your nervousness. Anyone can learn these techniques.

But the first thing which you have to accept is that if you are feeling nervous on the stage its absolutely okay, it's very natural. If you are not feeling nervous on the stage then there is a problem, that is very unnatural.

So don't worry about nervousness, don't avoid stage because of this. Because if you want to be a leader in your life you have to separate yourself from the crowd, stand alone and speak.

Chapter 6: Glossophobia Aka Fear Of Public Speaking

Before we can get you started putting together your presentation, let's try to figure out why you may have a fear of public speaking. It's the number one fear most Americans have, and it's called glossophobia. The second most-common fear is death. Think about that for a moment. Most people would rather die than speak publicly. Or you can look at it this way: at a funeral, most people would rather be the one in the casket than the one making the eulogy.

How does this fear develop? We are born with only two innate fears. They are the fear of falling and the fear of loud noises. Every other fear we have is learned. So, how do we learn them? Our prehistoric ancestors had some of the same fears we have now. And these fears, quite literally, saved their lives. They were afraid of heights, which kept them from falling off the edge of a cliff. They were afraid of spiders and snakes, which alleviated any curiosity about them. Our ancestors saw somebody fall off a cliff or have an extreme reaction to a bite from a spider, snake, or bug. And they learned to avoid them. Many of the fears we have protect us.

Most of our fears we develop through experiences that cause us stress. However, if you are afraid of spiders, snakes, water, heights, etc., and don't know why, they are most likely those primitive fears that protected others.

I have a friend named Eddie who was a Firefighter. This is a big, macho guy who is deathly afraid of snakes. If he sees a picture of a snake, he breaks into a cold sweat. In his profession, he had to go into all kinds of places where snakes can hide; under houses, into dark sheds, in the brush in the woods. Paramedics were on standby to manage his distress. He has never been bitten by a snake and he doesn't know anybody who has ever been bitten by a snake.

Fear prepares us to protect ourselves. Stay away from heights or you might fall. Stay away from the spider. You might get bitten. Stay out of the water. You might drown. Keep the lights on. You don't know what lurks in the dark.

So, what are we protecting ourselves from in front of a group? The reality is not that we have a fear of public speaking. We have a fear of rejection, being negatively judged by others and, ultimately, failure. We want to protect ourselves and our psyche.

Fears trigger a reaction of "what's the worst thing that can happen?" I fly a lot and do not understand the concept of jumping out of a perfectly good airplane. People do it all the time. Many people have done it and say it's one of the most exhilarating experiences of their lives. They will most certainly do it again. Have you seen the taped footage of this event? It scares me as much as public speaking might scare you. I truly see no thrill in it at all. The earth racing up to my face at ludicrous speed is terrifying. This is coming from somebody who enjoys life and engages in risky adventures. I love to scuba dive. I ride my own Harley-Davidson motorcycle and have gone on very long rides. But the thought of jumping out of that airplane with a parachute, that I'm hoping will open, absolutely terrifies me.

Most fears trigger the **ultimate** "worst thing that can happen": death. I've not heard or read of anybody dying from public speaking. So, let's try to determine what you're really afraid of. Your fear with public speaking could be any of the following: I'll forget what I was going to say or say the wrong thing. I'll make a joke and nobody will laugh. They'll think I'm stupid. They'll see me sweating. I won't be able to breathe. They won't like me. Very often, a person cannot tell me exactly why they are afraid. Most of the time they say everything about it scares them.

When I ask people why they fear public speaking, I've never had somebody respond, "I might die." It's the number one fear, yet it does not provoke the number one "worst thing."

To alleviate some of the fear associated with public speaking, the first step you must take is to narrow down the things you are afraid of and manage each one of these individually. Take a few minutes right now, put down the book, close your eyes and do your best to pinpoint your fear. Fear is an acronym for False Evidence Appearing Real. Your fear starts in your mind. You create your own worst case scenario. And if it starts with you, then you have the power to manage it your way.

Will you be nervous before you speak to a group of people EVERY TIME? I hope so. Nervousness is great energy when it's channeled correctly. I have never made a presentation where I was not nervous. Not one. Ever. There are many things you can do while preparing for your presentation that will create a more positive energy rather than a debilitating anxiety. The definition of anxiety is "looking forward to with dread." The definition of eager is "looking forward to with joy." The great thing about the human mind is that you can choose how you want to approach anything, and this includes public speaking.

Rather than focusing on the worst thing that can happen, you can help alleviate your fears by imagining the best thing that can happen. This single tip can change so many areas of your life.

Here are just a few better things to focus on:

I'll be successful.

The audience will understand what I'm saying.

I won't fall down and pass out.

I will be perceived as a knowledgeable professional.

I won't die.

There are very few opportunities in your adult life to impress others with the awesomeness that is you. You might be the best at what you do. Public speaking gives you the opportunity to show that to others.

Once you identify your fear and realize that it's very unlikely that it will come to fruition, and decide what the best thing is that can happen, it's time to create your expectation. I believe another obstacle to public speaking is that we set our expectations for success too high when we first do it. Here is yet another opportunity to begin with the end in mind. If you're looking for applause, create a presentation that provokes applause. If you're looking for a standing ovation, you better really bring it to the audience! Are you looking for laughter? Then create a presentation that will make people laugh. Will you hear snoring? Maybe. But if there is, that's not about you. Somebody in your audience didn't get enough sleep last night.

If you've never read the book, "The Four Agreements" by Don Miguel Ruiz, I suggest that you do. This single book changed my life. The second of the four agreements is "Don't Take Anything Personally." What people say about you is truly none of your business. It has more to do with them and their own experiences. Read the book. You'll thank me someday. All of the Four Agreements were created to help us live on this planet in a much more self-aware and reduced-stress frame of mind. If you really want to have a confidence level standing up in front of a group of people and making a presentation, this book will take you to a level that you did not realize you could attain.

Right now would be a great time for you to define success. Not in life or as a parent. How do you define success in public speaking? It's a point of reference that will change as your confidence level increases. There is a difference between confident and comfortable. One of the definitions of confident is the state or quality of being certain. One of the definitions of comfortable is free from stress. Let's get real; you will not be free from stress when you first start speaking in front of a group of people. But as you start to experience your best things that can happen, your stress level will decrease. The false evidence you perceived with the worst thing that can happen will start to subside. You will gradually take that stress and recognize it as positive energy that you can pass along to your audience.

The very first full-day seminar I presented as a Professional Speaker was one of the most nerve wracking days of my life. I had done keynote speeches, short presentations, and a couple of workshops. But now, this was my career.

I got to the conference room early and discovered that the Banquet Manager had set up chairs, but no tables. My anxiety level started to increase. You may have attended one of these seminars. The chairs were placed very close together. I immediately knew my challenge would be to keep these adults as comfortable as I could and engaged all day.

As soon as the participants arrived, they started complaining. My anxiety level increased. I was becoming highly stressed. They were trying to juggle their coffee and notebooks, while trying to get comfortable. They were verbally sharing their view of their day with each other, and it was not pleasant. Their anxiety was infectious, and began to spread throughout the room.

I was teaching a seminar on Priority Management. So, I started by addressing their issue (no tables, tight seating), telling them this would be a priority that we would manage throughout the day. I asked for a volunteer whose responsibility would be to give me a signal every 30 minutes. On that 30-minute mark, we would all get up and stretch for one-minute. I visibly saw the stress from the crowd decrease immediately. My anxiety level decreased at the same time.

At the end of the day, they were asked to fill out an evaluation of the seminar. There were two sections on the evaluation: the first was about the content of the seminar and the second was on the speaker. Remember it was the first one I'd ever done professionally and in front of a large crowd. Almost all of them commented on the uncomfortable setup of the room and almost all of them commented on how genuinely concerned I was with this and my solution to their problem. They also commented on how much they learned and how they could realistically apply the techniques at work and at home.

My expectation that I set in the morning was achieved. I kept them as comfortable as I could and they were engaged.

The expectation that most of us have is simply to create a presentation that we can get through with our dignity intact.

In my experience and in conversations that I have with people who are afraid of public speaking, I've discovered that the average person believes everybody that gets up and speaks is somehow born with the ability to do it. That, perhaps, the speaker is better than they are in some way; more talented, smarter, more attractive, or more charismatic. The reality is that nobody is better or worse than you…at anything. Everybody is simply different. I've discovered that people who become confident with public speaking are just exactly that; CONFIDENT! And the fastest and most effective way to build that confidence is to prepare, practice, and persevere.

As your confidence level climbs and you become more comfortable, you can change your expectations of your presentation.

Chapter 7: Defining The Purpose Of Your Speech

Speakers should understand precisely what they wish to put across. Therefore, before they actually begin to develop their presentations, many community speakers write an objective statement in which they specify their theme and establish the set of guidelines by which they will assess material that may be integrated in the presentation. If you have complications in defining the purpose of your speech, then the declaration that says exactly what the anticipated result of the presentation will be normally do not have a straightforward concept of what you are trying to point out. This comprises of three components: the objective of the presentation, the assertion of the subject matter, and the approach or process to be utilized to create the speech.

In all productive oratory, there should be an undoubtedly defined goal and purpose. The presenter should try to discover where his unique power lies and function in that course, always keeping in mind that the loftier the target the more significant the likely accomplishment. The objective of the presentation is decided by the kind of the speech. There are 4 distinct types of speeches you can present and their objective is to invoke diverse reactions.

An Informative Presentation is like teaching. The reason for an informative speech is to endeavor to teach a specific thing to the target audience. The achievement of the presentation you are giving is based on whether the crowd learns what you desired to teach them. You have to tell the crowd why the info is beneficial and valuable. You ought to ensure that the crowd understands and recalls the essential details.

A layout Presentation is compared to giving a person directions, or showing the location of a place through explaining. It is not very widely accepted as a formal presentation, but it is something you frequently have to when explaining to individuals regarding a town or huge building. This type of presentation tells the target audience where things are. It may as well describe their size and appearance.

Expressions are very crucial in a layout oral communication. In reality, this is a good opportunity to exercise your gestures. The triumph of your oral presentation is based on whether the listeners can discover their way around the area you have explained.

A demonstration speech is similar to an informative oral communication since you need to teach the target audience about a specific thing. Nevertheless, in this type of communication you will not just explain to the listeners about a specific thing, you will as well tell them how to perform the same. The presentation will be effective if at the conclusion of presentation the listeners can do what you taught them to do.

A persuasive speech includes information to guide individuals make a decision. The objective of a persuasive communication is to convince people to transform in some way. For instance, it could be changing the way they think about a specific issue or it could be changing their way of doing things.

Lastly, it could be to convince the listeners to carry out something that they know nothing about it. The oral presentation will be effective if at the closing stage of your presentation the listeners are ready to make the change you recommended.

Know what you would like to communicate to your target audience before you begin to organize your presentation. Figure out what you desire to accomplish. Concentrate on the objective of the presentation at every stage. This is to make sure that how you have prepared is appropriate and successful. In conclusion, defining the purpose of your speech is very important.

Chapter 8: How To Keep Your Audience Engaged, Excited And Entertained

As a Speaker, your primary role will be to keep your Audience Engaged, Excited and entertained in other for you to communicate your intended message to them. Below are tips and strategies you can employ to keep your audience engaged

1.   Tell stories

Storytelling is a crucial component of effective public speaking. It creates relevance for the audience, providing additional detail and mental visuals that bring to life otherwise dull, remote, or complex topics. Stories give speakers the opportunity to tell personal stories that relate to the audiences' experiences, thought processes, or values. Moreover, including stories in public speaking helps your audience to connect and engage emotionally with the speaker.

Ask questions during your presentation.

Incorporating questions in your presentations will help engage and involves your audience by stimulating their own thought processes. This technique also helps move between sections of your presentation as it establishes a clear transition from one point to another.

Invite people onto the stage

Always consider inviting your audience to come on stage and volunteer to share their experiences or undertake some fun-filled activities. This will help you grab their attention and bring in some new energy into the room

Use Ice Breakers

The best way to encourage a warm and friendly atmosphere is to get some kind of emotional response out of the audience right at the beginning. It doesn't matter what emotion it is, you just need to connect with them on a more personal level and you can do this by using ice breakers, if planned well, icebreakers are a great way to introduce participants to the event, clarify its objectives and create the right conditions to maximize their learning.

Practice your delivery

Public Speaking is all about practicing; try to always practice how to get the attention of your audience

Strong body language (position, posture, and gesture) one of the best ways to make your presentation interactive is to make your presentation lively and beautiful and you can go through your body language and the power of gestures. You shouldn't be afraid to use your arms and hands when talking as it makes you seem more passionate and confident.

Extend your vocal range You can use the tone and vocal variety of your voice to calm the emotions of your audience during a presentation, this can be achieved when you learn to project your voice high and low to stress some important points

Use Images and videos to grab attention

you can use powerful images or a 1-3 minute video to illustrate a point to get the attention of your audience

Maintain eye contact: Eye contact is a powerful communication tool that can help the speaker connect directly with the audience and communicate with them. Make sure to spread your eyes across the length and breadth of the room to catch a glimpse with your audience reactions during the presentation

Connect with the Audience by mentioning their names you can get your audience interactive by learning their names and using them during your presentations, I use this technique most often in my seminars to get audience concentration and also make them feel important

Make your presentation short and straight to the Point

Chapter 9: Walking Between A Ladder And A Wall

When you purchased this book, you had no idea that you would also be learning how to avoid bad luck for the rest of your life. Unfortunately, you will have to keep on guard at all times, as there is a lot more to avoid than just walking under a ladder.

I've done some of the heavy lifting for you and created a list of things to avoid if you are superstitious:

A black cat crossing one's path

Walking between a ladder and a wall

Certain numbers: 4,13,14, 666

Friday the 13th

Failing to respond to a chain letter

Breaking a mirror is said to bring seven years of bad luck

Shoes on a table

Opening an umbrella while indoors

Ravens, crows and magpies

If you may have encountered that black cat or broken a mirror, don't worry; here are a few things you can do to improve your odds:

Seeing a penny and picking it up daily

Knocking on wood

Breaking a wishbone and making a wish

Crossing your fingers

Taking a dead rabbit's foot around everywhere with you

Of course, these are all superstitions, however some of us have it so ingrained in our subconscious that we still wouldn't dare walk under the ladder!

I mean, life is a lot easier when you blame things that are within your control on external forces. Just ask your horoscope. Been having a tough time at work? Your car and washing machine break down in the same day? It's most likely because Mars is in retrograde.

I've seen people who have had a few things go wrong write off the entire year in June. #bringonthenewyear

So, what's this all got to do with public speaking?

Let me ask you this; where did you hear about all those good and bad luck superstitions? Who told you about star signs, horoscopes, and bad things happening in threes?

Can I hazard a guess and say it was your family, friends, and teachers?

Or as I like to call it society. The same society who taught your parents and their parents the same ideals.

When you hear it enough from a variety of people that it becomes ingrained in your subconscious, it changes your thoughts, feelings and emotions towards those things. You've been conditioned by society to walk, talk and act in a particular way.

Let me now ask you this; where did you first hear that public speaking was something that should be feared, that people hated it, that it's the biggest fear in the world?

I guarantee that as a child you didn't go to kindergarten and decide you wouldn't share at morning show and tell because you were meant to hate it.

Maybe your first experience was like mine; standing in front of an audience, trembling and panicked and unable to regain your confidence. Perhaps you have heard your parents, friends, or siblings complain about hating or dreading having to give a presentation.

"Whenever you find yourself on the side of the majority, it is time to pause and reflect."

– Mark Twain

So, if the majority is on the side of fearing and hating public speaking, is it time for us to pause and reflect?

To get better answers we need to ask better questions.

Why would we want to be a better public speaker?

For me, I have had different reasons at different stages in my life. Depending on your level of public speaking, you will probably go through a similar journey. In my early teenage years, I used it to build confidence and to gain an unfair advantage. Towards the end of my schooling years, I was using it to win school speech competitions, pass public speaking exams, and to qualify for national speech competitions to pit my skills against the best around.

Throughout my university years, I used it to nail presentations. Professionally, I have used it to confidently and more importantly effectively communicate with patients (I am a qualified Physiotherapist). Since then, I have further understood the power of public speaking to share a message with more people and have a greater impact. With the advancement of technology, the medium and reach is larger than ever before.

In the past, you traditionally had to speak live in front of people, being featured on radio or TV, or getting in print media to share your message. Nowadays you can be a micro-celebrity in any niche and tap into a worldwide market.

In the time of writing, you could be a podcaster, YouTuber, Facebook/Instagram/Snapchat influencer, or a gamer making money streaming and entertaining on Twitch. What is even more impressive is all of this can do done at low to no cost from the comfort of your own home. All these mediums both new and old can create opportunities into other complimentary spaces as well.

Take for example my journey with my first podcast, "The Youngpreneurs Podcast". It successfully launched to #1 on iTunes New and Noteworthy in six different countries. This was done with no previous broadcasting experience, no list or following, in a niche I had never been in.

This put me on the radar. Not on the Oprah or Ellen show radar, but it started a chain of events. Within six weeks I was being invited to speak at online summits, and my guests were paying me to help them set up successful podcasts as a service. I created a training company off the back of it.

Other podcasters wanted to feature my story on their show, and I was encouraged to write a book, "The Authority Handbook"; connecting with some of the world's biggest influencers such as Grant Cardone. I participated in multiple media appearances, and got invited to talk at international podcast events, which resulted in an invite to speak at a TEDx event.

Public Speaking is no longer for just the boardroom, politicians and motivational speakers like Tony Robbins.

A lot of you might not want to be a TEDx speaker, podcaster or international speaker, but the thing is, the ability to confidently present and speak applies to whatever you do. It's the fastest way to build authority, highlight your expertise and to get people to know, like, and trust you.

We live in a busy world. The saying is time is money. I personally think time is a lot more precious than money. It is a non-renewable resource that once we use it, whether that be productively or non-productively, it's gone.

Speaking allows leverage of your time. There is obviously a time for one to one meetings, consultations and promotion. The ability to do this on a one to many scale will amplify your effectiveness.

The scaling of communication looks something like this:

1-to-1: In most cases, it's a high time commitment if you aim to impact a lot of people. This should be reserved for your highest paying clients, as your time is precious.

1-to-many: Speaking to a boardroom, pitching to multiple investors, running group training, speaking at events.

0 to many: This is my personal favourite. This is when you create a piece of content (blog podcast, podcast, recorded training, deliver a keynote, host a webinar), and that training can then be used repeatedly 24/7. I know of business owners who have created successful sales webinars that they have then run on auto-pilot to generate multiple seven figures. The focus here shouldn't be on the money; however, if you want to make more money, positively impact more people. If that webinar involves selling a training or service that then allows more people to do better, then money is just the by-product.

Think of the case of a personal trainer friend of mine, Sean. Personal trainers generally get into the industry because they like fitness and want to help people create and live healthier lives. Sean was the same. He started in his first gym and quickly got a good name for himself, and business was good. Then comes the realisation that there are only so many hours in the day to work with people one to one.

He transitioned his business to create a mix of higher priced 1-to-1 sessions and began to offer small group training and boot camps. He was now impacting more people and generating more revenue.

The same problem occurs though; only so many hours in the day. The only option to level up was more of the 1-to-many group classes. Instead of just creating more group exercise classes, he decided to use public speaking for leverage with fitness education classes.

Working on goals and accountability in a group, bringing in dieticians, physio's, and physiologists to run some of these sessions did three things.

Allow his clients to get a better overall experience.

Leverage his time to talk 1-to-many for a lot of the things he was previously doing 1-to-1.

Bring in other experts, which boosts his authority.

Guess what then happened? He maxed out his time again. He had to devise a strategy to leverage more 0 to many options and pick the highest yielding 1 to many options to have a bigger impact.

For many of the business minded out there, the answer is clear; hire trainers to run the groups. The result was that his 1-to-1 time was spent training his trainers, and 1-to-many was spent delivering presentations to organisations about the benefits of exercise, which positioned him and his company as authorities in the space and ensured a steady flow of new clients.

With new trainers onboard, he was having a fitness impact on a 0 to many scale, was generating more $$$'s, and had more time. This time lead to an online training platform which he uses public speaking skills to run webinars, create online training programs and impact even more people worldwide.

This all sounds like smooth sailing, but a lot of his success can be attributed to improving his public speaking skills and having the ability to succinctly convey that he could solve his potential client's problems. As he improved his speaking he could now rinse and repeat the speech to different audiences and leverage his time and maximize his impact.

"All things being equal, people will do business with and refer business to, those people they know like and trust"

– Bob Burg

We are in the most exciting era ever known to man. Gone are the days when to get known you needed to appear in a T.V. feature, on the radio or spend tens of thousands of dollars to get known.

Around 40% of the world has access to the internet, which is much more than the 1%

in 1995. With the technological advancements that companies like Facebook and Google are putting out, it is estimated that by 2025 every person in the world will have access to the internet.

Let's me ask you a question. With over seven billion people in the world set to have access to the online world, what percentage of that pie would you need to 10X (even 100x) your business?

Here's the unfortunate thing; just because all these people are coming online, doesn't mean that more are going to be following you, using your products or services, or becoming raving fans.

There is, however, a tried and tested way to get in front of more people and get them in a state they were they want to follow you, learn from you, buy off you, and refer you to friends. This three-step technique that moves your audience through a straightforward process of know-like-trust. This isn't just for the online world, it's for live talks, business proposals, making friends and dating.

Before anyone will make any type of deep commitment to you, be that accepting an idea, purchasing a product or service, hiring you for a job, or saying yes to that first date, most people will want to at least know who you are. The basis is simply this; if people don't know you how can you expect to want to do business with you?

Becoming known partly comes back to how you position yourself, build your authority, and highlight your expertise which all tie into people liking you more and trusting you.

Think if you were looking for an accountant. There are three in your area all with similar qualifications and have been in business for a similar amount of time. You happen to go to a local event where one of the accountants is presenting some helpful tips for tax time.

They are now on your radar; you know who they are. They then give you some amazing tips and show their expertise. This giving of value has led you to like them. You are then discussing them with one of your friends who raves about how great they are. This recommendation from an independent third party creates enough trust for you that it's a no-brainer.

Getting in front of their target market at an event allowed them to be at the front of the mind and be known. Giving value allowed them to be liked and build some trust. The trust was then drummed home with a recommendation from your friend.

It's important to begin to understand you are an expert. My personal definition is you are an expert if you can teach 8/10 people walking down the street something about your chosen topic or area of expertise. Once you believe you are an expert in the subject you now must become the expert in presenting it.

Being trained as a physiotherapist, I think I am an expert in the rehabilitation of injuries. Sure, there are lecturers, professors and world leaders who have more expertise than me; they are the experts to the experts; but I can still bring immense amounts of value to the general population.

Stop what you are doing, and I want you to write down a list of all the things you believe yourself to be an expert in based on my definition.

It's surprising just how many things you have a level of expertise in isn't it?

The problem is, many experts are the best-kept secret.

As experts, we need to be building up our authority in that industry. Whether that's speaking at events, creating a blog or podcast, featuring in the media, interviewing other industry leaders, or creating referral partners and raving fans.

Think back to the last person you heard speak from the stage, host a tv show or train you at a workplace. By being the centrepiece presenting, they command authority which, if done well, with further enhance your business and brand.

Getting people to commit to doing any type of business with you is more than just having the best product or being the smartest in your industry. Authority building exercises get you in front of and known by more of your ideal people, which allows you to highlight your expertise and lets them like and trust you.

Authority + Expertise = Attention + Trust + Opportunities

In a dopamine fixated world with the attention span of a goldfish, being an effective public speaker who can hold people's attention while conveying a message is gold. The mediums might change over time, but the fundamental philosophies stay the same.

Warren Buffett, one of the wealthiest and most successful people of this generation, ranks it as the most important skill you can invest in for your future success. The only thing he has framed in his office is a certificate he received from public speaking training he did in the 1950's.

He even goes onto say he would pay 10% of your future earnings and that you can improve your value by 50% by learning communication skills and public speaking.

That should be a compelling reason as any. Let's dive into the strategies that will allow you to quickly and effectively improve your speaking skills and confidence.

Chapter 10: Understanding The Elements Of Public Speaking

In this chapter, you will be able to understand the communication pattern that is usually followed in the field of public speaking. In order to understand this pattern, you will need to dissect the elements that are involved every time a speaker talks in front of a large audience. There are five elements of public speaking and each will be explained briefly in this chapter.

Element of Public Speaking #1: Speaker

The speaker is considered as the second most important factor in any speech. The most important, of course is your speech. Others refer to the speaker as the sender. The sender is a person who sends and encodes a certain message. He directs it to the receiver using a certain medium or channel. Therefore, the sender or the speaker is the creator of any communication cycle.

When a speech is crated, the speaker encodes a message. After that, the audience will decode the speech's message. They decode using their intellect, observation, and experience. They look out for clues from the manner of your delivery to aid them in the process of decoding.

Element of Public Speaking #2: Message

It does not matter what communication model you follow. In any case, you will find out that the most important element in the process of communication is the message. Without any message, communicating with an audience is not possible. The word message came from a Latin word that literally means "to send."

In the arena of public speaking, the speech is the message. It bears your intention as well as your goal. Usually, a speech, regardless of its length converges at a particular point, emotion, or goal.

As the writer and delivery medium of the speech, you should also make it a point to make an effort to understand the message from your audience. This way, you can send a message in response to what they have sent. Therefore, the exchange of messages becomes more and more complex until the distinction of "sender" and "receiver" disappears.

Remember that a message can be sent by verbal and non-verbal means. While words are the easiest to understand, other cues that are non-verbal by nature like eye contact, gestures, and postures also send significant messages which in turn are decoded by your audience. With that, both should be used in the process of crafting your speech.

Element of Public Speaking #3: Channel

Claude Shannon crafted the SMCR model of communication. SMCR stands for sender, message, channel, and receiver. Shannon defined channel as the medium by which the message was sent by the sender to the receiver. For example, if the situation is a face-to-face conversation, the medium is audio using the sound you produce and the visuals using the light waves around you. However, if you make a call via Skype, the medium or channel is computer-aided visual and audio.

Element of Public Speaking #4: Audience

According to experts, the audience is the third most important element in the process of communication. Demographics refer to the characteristics of a certain audience – their distinguishing traits and their common features. As a crafter of the message, it is a big no-no to stereotype your audience. You should take the demographics of your audience seriously. Aristotle once said that in order to succeed in public speaking, you should know your audience. This is a universal truth in the world of communication.

There are several factors that you should consider when you confront or approach any audience:

Ø Age: As a crafter of the audience, you should research on the age range of the group. Also, you should have the knowledge about their age gaps as well. Though they say that age is just a number, but it can give you a lot of information about the people you are talking to. Their degree of understanding of different things in the society and in history depends on age. If you know what is their knowledge base, you will know what kind of input (that you can integrate in your speech) that they can process.

Ø Race and Culture: These two characteristics are separate things, but they complement each other and depend on one another. By studying the race and culture of your audience, you will know what facial expressions, words and gestures that may be offensive to them. Also, you will know the appropriate manner of conveying your message by looking closely at their culture and race.

Ø Gender: You should also know whether your audience is dominated by men or women. If the audience is predominantly male, there is a specific approach. If the audience is predominantly female, another approach might work better.

Ø Educational Attainment and Occupation: If possible, you should request this information from the organizer of the event. This bit of information will help you determine what kind of language may work and what level of information that they can appreciate and understand.

Element of Public Speaking #5: Feedback

Feedback is an element that is integrated in advanced communication models. It refers to the return message or response given by the receiver directed to the sender of the original message. For example, after holding a speech, an evaluation can be made by the organizers to gauge the audience's degree of liking in connection to your presentation. However, it may not be that formal – you can receive feedback if you are observant enough. Audience members laughing, nodding, and yawning – all of these are different forms of feedback.

As a speaker, you should open your eyes, ears, heart, and mind to the different kinds of feedback that may come your way. This way, you can do the necessary adjustments to improve the audience's way of receiving the message that you deliver.

Element of Public Speaking #6: Noise and Interference

Noise, in the context of communication, pertains to something unpleasant or jarring that can interrupt or distract the communication process. These are road block that prevent the message from being delivered properly from the sender to the receiver. In the context of public speaking, noise and interference can be a major concern because it might compromise the message.

Noise does not necessarily pertain to the noise as we know it. It can refer to something internal or external. Based on experience, external noise are easier to manage. It is easier to replace a malfunctioning microphone. It is easy to deal with chatting members of the audience. These are two examples of external noise. Internal noise is more challenging because it can be psychological as opposed to external noise which is usually physical. Some examples of internal noise are stress, nervousness, and anxiety.

Chapter 11: Structure Of The Presentation

A well balanced presentation or a speech has three main parts as: Introduction, Body & Conclusion.

Developing body

☐ Body or the main content of the speech/presentation must have more than 3 (three) & less than 5 (five) main points. Less than 3 main points will make your content too small as a speaker while more than 5 will make it too big to be absorbed by the audience. The structure of the body should be well organized & balanced so that it helps to maintain the interest throughout the entire period of your speech. Each & every sub topics, examples, statistics or the illustrations must be related to the main concept of the content.

☐ The well-organized structure falls into one of the following categories. If anyhow, the body structuring of the speech or the presentation does not fall into one specific pattern, then you should make some adjustments to make it into a single one. These categories are:

Chronological

The chronological pattern likely to discuss steps or processes or series of events related to a main concept in a chronological order.

Example: Steps to improve public speaking skills

Spatial structuring

Spatial structuring involves the discussion of various parts of a specific area & how they work together to form the whole concept.

Example: Structure of a speech: Introduction, body & conclusion

Topical

Topical structuring involves the discussion of various categories of a particular area.

Example: Five types of visual aids in public speaking.

Problem solving

This type of structuring involves the discussion of a particular problem & its solution.

Example: How to avoid anxiety in public speaking

Cause & effect

Cause & effect structuring involves the discussion of causes & its effect on the environment & on the people.

Example: Why not to avoid public speaking

Contrast

Contrast structuring is used to pointing out the differences between various concepts related to a particular area.

Example: Power point v/s hand-outs in public speaking

Comparison

Comparison structuring is the opposite of contrast structuring. It is used to point out the similarities between various concepts of an area.

Example: Power point & visual aids for public speaking

Refutation

Refutation structuring involves in pointing out the valid points of an established argument.

Example: one cannot deny that.... (Your view)

Developing introduction

☐   Introduction should always be made according to the main body of the speech or the presentation. This is the most important part of your speech & used up to gain audience attention from the very first.

☐   It should be well organized & should able to give good impression to the audience. In this part, your main task is to disclose the topic of your speech or presentation. Hence, it should be well understandable by the audience.

☐   Besides, you should provide some good reasons to the audience about why they should listen to you? What will be the benefits of your presentation topic? Your introduction should be the best part of your entire work so that you get the full attention of your audience.

How to develop a breath-taking introduction

☐ Keep your introduction brief & touchy. Avoid making the introduction part too long. This way you will lose your audience attention & your self-confidence as well. A good introduction must not be more than 10-15% of the total speech contents.

☐ To make your introduction interesting, you can include a short story in the very beginning of your speech. This way you can get a lot of attention from the audience. You can also opt for a story that starts at the very beginning & ends in the ending part of your speech or presentation.

☐ Using some kind of shocking statistics in the introduction part may also be useful to get audience attention. However, make sure to put accurate & easily understandable points so that everyone can understand it without any prior knowledge.

☐ Try to relate the theme of your speech to the daily facing problems by the people & tell them how your speech can help them to get over it.

Developing conclusion

☐ The last part of the presentation or the speech is the conclusion. It should be well organized just like the introduction & the body part of your speech.

☐ Every conclusion must give a review of the speech & should give a little glimpse of the main concept of your speech.

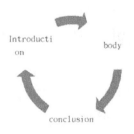

Introduction   body

conclusion

☐ Try to avoid putting new information in the conclusion part. Follow the round structure technique in a speech that is the content interconnects the introduction, body & conclusion part for an effective speech.

☐ While the introduction part is the preview of the main body content, the conclusion part must give the review of the same. It should also provide the solution to any stated problem in your speech & also talk about under what circumstances the main idea of the speech can be beneficial.

Final assembly of speech

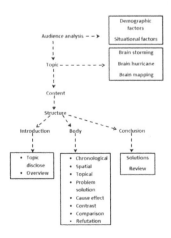

Chapter 12: Why Public Speaking Is Scary And The Science Behind It

Are you scared of delivering speech, presentation or even communicating with your fellow peers? I don't know about you but lot of people are facing this challenge. And creating and delivering speeches that connects with an audience and causes change to happen is not luck. It is a science, techniques, or strategy if applied can unlock your fear of public speaking.

As you can see the fear of public speaking also called "glossophobia" is a type of anxiety similar to stage fright with symptom such as feeling of impending doom, obsessive taught of fear or worry, palms sweating, weaken and cracked voice, trembling and shaking, dizziness, sweating, nausea, accelerated heartbeat, and dry mouth.

If any of the above indicates you, listen carefully nothing is wrong with you, you are only passing through emotion of public speaking which the consequences can result to the above. But don't worry the solution you've looking for is here.

I was once a victim and it was terrible until I decided to take "responsibility" of my actions. Take note of the word "responsibility" meaning response + ability. Your ability to respond to emotions such as fear and anxiety.

In other words, if you can take mastery of the emotions you respond to, then you are one step away to mastering your fear of public speaking. I will explain more about this in upcoming chapter.

Each time you think of negative consequences or response, a part of your brain known as hypothalamus activates and trigger's the pituitary gland that secrets the hormone ACTH. This hormone stimulates the adrenal gland in your kidney as result in the release of adrenaline into your blood stream.

At this point in time, most of us experience reactions and begins to respond to it. In the process, your neck and your back muscle begins to contract (forcing your head down and your spine to curve) moving your posture into a slouch.

This result in low-power position as your body tries to force itself into the fetal position.

At this stage if you try to resist the position such as pulling your shoulder backward and lifting up your head, you'll notice your hands and your legs begins to shake, with tension all over your body as the muscle in your body instinctively prepare for an impending attack.

What happens next is that your blood pressure accelerates and your digestive system shuts down to maximize efficient delivery of more oxygen and nutrients to your vital organs.

Also the shutting down of the digestive system leads to feelings of dry mouth or butterflies and in most cases causes your pupils to dilate, making it difficult to read any close material such as your presentation note, thereby expands your long range visibility, alerting you of your audience facial expressions.

At this point you are gripped with much more fear which could lead to temporary depression and it seems like all the information you have rehearsed and known very well, has just gone whirling away with your confidence leaving you empty. Still staring at the anticipating audience, and all you really want to do is flee.

Hello are you scared of what's happening inside of you? don't be, remember you are not alone. I have suffered the symptoms too until my solution came through. Which i will share with you in this book to enable you breakthrough public speaking phobia.

I will never forget the day I defended my high school internship project at a community clinic. All participants and trainees where gathered in an auditorium sitting side by side in a circle.

One after the other introducing ourselves with, name, school attended and interesting facts about us. I was so tense, I was fearful and worry, I could hardly breath as if the roof will collapse on me, my voice cracked internally with my shoulder down, with constant sweating, trembling and shaking.

I couldn't even hold my pen and paper firmly. My mouth was warbling as if drenched by the rain. My heart rate accelerated and was panting faster like someone who took 500-meter race.

Other intense noticed my fear but hardly said anything. Anyway thank God I'm second to the last in the list, I said. I sat there festering until it was my turn. I could hardly even listen to other presenters as it got closer to mine.

I was filtering my taught all alone in my head, what will I say? Immediately I looked at the nest presenter as everyone in the room clapped him with trembling voice, congratulating his performance.

He is far more confident and better looking than me, I concluded. Let's welcome the nest presenter Scott Reynolds. Immediately I heard my name, my heart jumped into my stomach, with instant wrinkles all over my face, I was frozen like a jelly fish.

Am gone I said. i stood up, make eye contact and gave my presentation in cracked flat monotone voice.

"I'm. I'm. I'm... Scott Reynolds"

I stammered while pronouncing my name, and at the end of the presentation, I concluded i make fool of myself, as no one clapped or praised my effort. Instead I was hearing negative comments of how I wad fidgeting.

While I sat down with wrinkles and anger all over my forehead, all I was thinking in my head was failure, failure, failure.

That was indeed a horrible experience of my life and in that moment I made a decision that "I Scott Reynolds will never engage in any stupid or destructive emotion of public speaking".

Could you believe that this single decision changed my life? At that moment I started consuming any information that could enhance my public speaking skills, I watche videos on YouTube, and read 100's of books and articles, including Tony Robbins: awaken the giant within, and other important books he wrote.

I visited self-development blog including project life mastery. I attended public speaking seminars. Anything that could help me, I did undermining the cost.

One thing is sure, if I can't stop this stupid emotion of public speaking now, then everything in my life is ruined, including my relationship, health and finance.

Because at that point of my life i couldn't communicate with opposite sex. My longtime girlfriend left me, not because i wasn't providing for her but because I couldn't communicate her needs effectively, and the relationship was boring.

I felt lonely with few friends, just like me beside me. I settled for less than I could become because I was scared of going for job interviews with high payout.

But today, everything has turned around with one simple decisions "I will never engage in any stupid or destructive emotion of public speaking". presently am a prolific public speaker both in marriage ceremonies, community programs, church programs, seminars, anything that involves public speaking, call me I will answer you.

Right now I don't know much about you or what you are passing through. Is the fear of public speaking holding you back in any area of your life? Or is speaking in front of groups scares you?

The truth is if you can analyze your fear and face it by making decision today, you will be able to communicate and engage audience with enthusiasm, confidence, passion. And all these you will discover as you turn to the nest chapter.

Chapter 13: What To Do During D-Day

Dress for Confidence

Wear something comfortable during D-Day. It can be your favorite suit or dress. Just make sure that you look good in front of the audience and you feel good inside. Dressing well helps boost your confidence levels. Wearing something uncomfortable will only increase your anxiety. You're already feeling unwell inside, you don't want uncomfortable clothing to aggravate your situation. Besides putting on your best clothes will make you feel more in control of yourself knowing that you look good in front of a crowd. Good clothes just have that kind of powerful mental impact.

Take Time to Interact with Your Audience

Educators from The University of California, Berkeley, suggest that it will help to boost your confidence if you speak to people in the audience before the time you actually deliver your speech. You can walk around the room to greet and chat with the early birds. It will help the audience become more receptive to you. They will get to see your more human features and remove some of the mysticism between you and your audience.

By the time you are to give your speech you would have won the hearts of some of the audience even before you have delivered your message. Other than being a good way to distract you from the stress of public speaking, by the time you speak your first line at the microphone you know that you're delivering your message in front of friends and not complete strangers.

Increase the Positive Pep-Talk

Authorities from Winthrop University suggest that it will help boost your confidence if you give yourself a round of positive pep talk. During the minutes before you actually deliver your speech, remember to smile. Envision how great will be your delivery only minutes from now. Imagine how relaxed your posture should be. Remind yourself that everyone in this room thinks that you are an eloquent speaker and that they are proud of you. They now eagerly await for whatever it is that you have to say.

Give the Adrenaline a Way Out

If the butterflies in your stomach and the shaking just won't go away within minutes of your talk then go to the men's room or ladies room and allow yourself to blow some steam. Remember that when your body pumps adrenaline it is trying to prepare for a perceived attack. Shake it off, walk around, jump up and down, wrinkle and twist your face in front of a mirror.

The important thing is to let your body burn up the adrenaline and allow your body to let your mind take the wheel and the driver's seat. The important thing is for you to find an outlet for the adrenaline rush. Once you have all of that out of the way then you can do a better job at delivering your message to your audience.

Never Ever Apologize

A lot of first time speakers make this cardinal mistake when giving a talk to an audience or congregation. Never ever apologize to the crowd. That ruins everything including the wonderful introduction that was written and read in front of the audience. Most of all, don't apologize to the audience about being nervous. Take note that nobody has even noticed that you were nervous – well that was until the time that you apologized about being nervous, now everybody knows.

Do you think that that will help you gain confidence? Will that make the crowd any less forgiving? Now that you have called the attention of the audience to your current anxiety anything extra that you do will be interpreted as being nervous.

Never apologize about anything whether it is in the lack of your preparation, being forced to deliver an impromptu speech, or being less confident and anxious about public speaking. History has shown that it will never help your cause. It's not even going to help you become more confident.

The Show Must Go on Even if You Blush in Public

Okay, so other than making you look a little cute in front of a live audience, what else does blushing do to you? That's right! Absolutely nothing. No one in the audience will really care if you turn slightly pinkish as you deliver your speech. Someone in the audience may snap a couple of pictures of you in case they think you're perfect for the role of the next pop icon. But other than that you don't really have to worry. The blushing will die down eventually and the world will go on its merry little way.

Take Shelter

When your hands begin to shake beyond your control remember that it's time to take shelter. Find something firm to hold and grip it firmly until your hands stop shaking. Don't grab the microphone. Chances are it will shake along with your hands. A better option is to grab hold of the podium away from the sight of the audience. Grab on tightly until your shaking abates. This is also a time for you to multitask. While grabbing a firm hold of the podium keep on talking. Remember that the show must go on.

Of course, you can move around in your presentation. You should have pre-arranged everything when you made your preliminary visit. You can have a table set up where the projector is and that can be a place where you can "hide" from the audience for a few minutes as you run the slides in your discussion. The podium, a table, and a few sections of the stage can serve as your safety zones where you can feel that you are safe from the scrutiny of your audience. Use these shelters to ease the tension you are feeling inside.

Finish Off with the Most Important Points First – No Need to Stave Off the Inevitable

If you are one of the speakers in a series, ask if you can go first. Have you noticed how waiting all this time for your chance at delivering the message is fueling your anxiety? Well then, why not arrange for you to go first and get done with it, right? It will help you get over your nerves and eventually enjoy the messages from the other speakers.

In case it's your turn to speak make sure that you bring up your main points near the beginning of your message. Remember that the attention of your audience is at their highest at the very beginning of your talk. Remember to bring them up again somewhere in the middle and close your talk by reemphasizing your main points at the end. Don't worry so much about losing your audience somewhere along the way. That's just how the human attention span works. The audience will eventually be able to catch up with you and put things together as they pay more attention once more.

Slow Down

One reaction that people have when they are getting nervous during a speech is that they tend to speak too fast. It's as if they want to get done with the dirty business as fast as they can. In case you notice that you are already pacing too fast in your speech do this: pause for emphasis, breathe in deep, hold it while looking at your audience (as if further emphasizing your point), exhale slowly, and then continue your speech – this time take on a slower pace.

Get the Right Picture

Do you think that you already look nervous? Do you think that someone in the audience has noticed that you already appear like a nervous wreck? Remind yourself not to worry. You actually look good on the outside. You only look like a nervous wreck on the inside. You can never look as nervous as you actually feel inside.

Pick Out the Friendly Faces in the Crowd

If you have friends coming over to listen to you message then figure out where they are sitting. When you deliver your speech look at them directly and speak to them head on. It will give an impression of confidence and it will also boost your confidence and enhance your delivery. Scan the audience and look for faces that you may not know but looks friendly in any case. Speak to them directly for a few seconds and then let go.

In case you're still a bit jittery about looking people in the eye then there's no harm in missing the target a bit – look at their foreheads! At least you are helping them and helping yourself in the process. Keep practicing that until you gain enough confidence to look people in the eye when delivering your speech.

Wear a Stress Saver

Bring or wear a token of someone who supports you. It can be a ring, a tie, a pen, or that laser pointer thingy that you can use to point out items in the overhead projection. At any rate, make sure that your token is something that means so much to you. It can be your wedding ring to remind you that your wife is there to support you in this effort. It can be that laser pointer that your professor gave you for good luck. These things can help you get your mind right back on track and give you a boost in your confidence level.

What to Do After the Speech

Take note that your speech doesn't actually end after you have spoken you concluding lines and taken your seat. Some of the people in the audience may want to congratulate you or at least greet you. Well, give them that chance. Oh, there's a chance that you'll hear a mix of both good and bad. Don't let that bother you. Remember to be kind to everyone especially yourself. Acknowledge that there were lapses in your speech. Well, the truth is that it can happen to anybody – even to the president of the United States giving his State of the Union speech.

The next step is to evaluate your speech. Enumerate the good things that you did and identify the mistakes you made. Emphasize your strong points and pat yourself in the back. Find out how you can avoid making the same mistakes twice.

Remember not to be too tough on yourself. There will always be room for improvement. Let your experiences build you and eventually it will fuel your confidence the next time you have to give a talk in front of a crowd.

Finally, after all the evaluations are done go out and reward yourself for your current achievements. Let this remind you that public speaking is a rewarding experience. With every speaking engagement comes a reward.

Chapter 14: Should I Outline My Most Important Points?

Okay. I already answered this, but yes. You should outline your most important points. It's good information if you use a handout, and it helps you find your place if you get lost in the speech. Many speakers will use PowerPoint to do this, and I've seen it work fine, and I've seen it turn into a nightmare as the speaker loses her place or can't get the PowerPoint to open and she has no idea where to go. Be careful of crutches. If someone kicks them away, you want to be able to keep going.

Should I Use Notes?

Sure. Use notes if you need them. But sometimes they are more trouble than they are worth – trying to figure out where to hide them, how to see them, etc. But sometimes we need that security. And your audience isn't going to mind if you're holding a note in your hand. Big deal. I would rather you hold notes than lose your place and start crying and put yourself and the audience through a miserable experience.

How Do I Address A Hostile Group?

I guess it depends on how hostile. If they're raging drunk and throwing stuff at you, you might want to think about leaving. And whatever you do, don't show anger or hostility in return. Rise above it. The audience won't appreciate the heckler, but if you turn on the heckler, then that same audience will turn on you.

I haven't ever been in a hostile audience as a motivational speaker. Worst thing I've faced is bad evaluations, people who don't laugh, or people who don't seem really interested in what I have to say. At first it stung to come across people who didn't like me. And then I got over it. This world is made up of lots of different types of people. We don't all like the same things. We don't like the same music. We like different TV shows. We all dress differently. It only makes sense that you won't please everybody.

The 10/10/80 Rule

10% of your audience will not like you because they don't like anybody. 10% will love you because they love everybody. 80% will wait and see what you have to say, and then decide. Your goal is to please 80% of your audience. If you're not doing that, then you have more work to do.

How Do I Overcome The Tendency To Say Um and Uh?

Oddly enough, we don't say "um" and "uh" when we speak with our friends. Yet in some speakers, these words run rampant in their speeches. It's because we use these words when we don't know what to say – when we are at a loss for words. It's also a nervous habit, which comes out when we're nervous. And most people speaking in front of a group are nervous. So it's normal. But not okay. It is very annoying to an audience and a sign that you aren't a professional. So get them out of your speech.

How? By writing your speech and memorizing every word. The more you know your speech, the less you find yourself at a loss for words. You'll probably still throw a couple of "ums" in there (habits take a while to break) but eventually they will disappear.

Where Do I Look During a Presentation?

You look at the audience. Sounds like a no-brainer, but you would be surprised how many people don't.

Try not to look at your notes the whole time. We don't want to stare at the top of your head. And while it's okay to look at your Power Point, it's not okay to spend the whole time looking at it. I once watched a speaker's Power Point fail (happens all the time) and she actually looked at the audience and said, "Wow! I'm not used to looking at you! This feels weird."

In order to connect to your audience they have to feel like you are talking to them. So you must look at them. Don't stare at one person to the point they feel uncomfortable. Look around the room, making eye contact as you go. Include everybody, even if you can't see them all. Look at all the corners, the front, the sides, the back, etc. You never want a part of the audience to feel like you are leaving them out.

If you are really nervous, then stare at the top of their heads. They won't know that you aren't actually looking them in the eyes.

Chapter 15: More About Wardrobe & Nerves

For some years I was fortunate to have a manager (a very senior academic) who believed in giving staff opportunities to try new skills. Unfortunately, this particular boss was also inclined not to provide much, or any, notice of the opportunity (nor brook a refusal). Some could call it baptism by fire. At the very least he saved you all that fret and worry which comes from too much preparation time. Good of him really.

The particular occasion I have in mind was at a postgraduate alumni event. It was being held at a fancy location, special guests, high-flying alumni, executives, top shelf horses doovers (hors d'oeuvres). The evening consisted of the usual haphazard arrival of guests, distribution of name tags, welcome announcement, wine, up-market nibbles, speeches, back slapping hail well met - the usual thing. As part of my new role, I had organised the event and fortunately it was going well.

I've just remembered an amusing incident from that evening. Still makes me smile. The deep fried morsels had been rapidly and enthusiastically consumed, in quantities by a couple of female guests. I had been chatting to them and the wait staff didn't pass them without their load of deep-fried goodies being considerably reduced. Nothing wrong with that. I had stopped to talk just as savoury nibbles were replaced by the sweet. A plate of yummy looking creamy things arrived. The two young women both looked askance at the waiter as if he was serving something quite disgusting, and one said "no thanks, we are both on a diet". Good grief.

The evening event was drawing to a close and my nerves were finally starting to settle. The life of the event manager is one of risk management, rapid problem solving - and moments of sheer panic. No-one notices when it all goes well but sure will complain when it doesn't. I was on the downhill run. Breathing again.

The last agenda item was for my boss to thank all for their attendance and bid them a safe drive home. Silly me. Nothing so simple. My boss decided that THIS was the time for me to start developing my public speaking skills. That is to say he didn't ask - he just expected me to do it. A cranky but kind-hearted conundrum of a boss he had high expectations of himself and everyone else. Excuses rarely ever got me (or anyone else) anywhere and getting out of a task just because I hadn't done it before was not gaining any ground at all.

It was my first foray into closing an event and it just happened to be at a high-powered cocktail function with a couple of guests of some distinction and others who I worked with.

All that was required was to breathe deeply. Walk up the stairs to the raised podium. Just remain vertical. DON'T WET YOUR PANTS! I instructed myself. This was my first public speaking event in front of people who knew stuff and got paid a lot for knowing stuff.

I covered the usual recognition of dignitaries and presented gifts to those who had spoken during the evening, proposed "thank-yous" to special guests, announced the next event, and wished them a safe drive home. I looked down at the sea of faces and felt overwhelmed. Had what I said made any sense at all? Was it all just in my head? This activity was so far outside my comfort zone. Still no-one was throwing anything towards me other than friendly faces or the random disinterested, glazed look. Perhaps that was the free alcohol. I left the podium.

Now it was the unfortunate consequence of my fear and loathing of public speaking at the time that any food or drink I had consumed had the unfortunate habit of going through my digestive system at a rapid rate. Since finding employment in the corporate world, sudden visits to the ladies room were par for the course, even at the possibility of talking to more than three senior people at a time or stating my name at a meeting. This particular event was certainly no exception. The end of the event meant an urgent need for a quick exit. I moved rapidly through the dispersing crowd. The other good thing about toilets is that they also offer privacy and a place to recover and collect one's composure.

I looked down. My fly was undone!

Okay it was a pants suit – and yes, they were fashionable for a brief moment in time.

Lesson 10 – Reduce the risk of malfunctions by managing your wardrobe in advance.

Take appropriate steps to reduce the risk (and associated stress) to avoid anything that might cause wardrobe malfunctions. The important thing is comfort, reliability, stain resistant fabric, working zippers, firmly sewn buttons, and shoes that don't pinch and can navigate stairs.

What should you wear for your first or next presentation?

Whatever is right for you and that requires the least risk management. This is not about fashion statements but how to reduce the chances that your nerves will not be helped by sweaty under arms, coffee stains, broken zips, tight pants, and more. Check for buttons that might pop open and show more than acceptable cleavage (or chest hair), wear heels that won't get caught in carpet tears, hosiery without ladders, and avoid jewellery that might better suit a belly dancing class.

Coco Chanel is quoted as advising the following when dressing with accessories:

"Before you leave the house, look in the mirror and take one thing off."

Wear something that hides a multitude of life's stains (the spill of that last minute caffeine fix, the child up-chuck just as you were leaving the house and the drips resulting from washing your hands - and then discovering the loo hand drier doesn't work).

Don't forget to wear comfortable and polished shoes - preferably not new shoes that might pinch.

Making a personal statement of who you are is important but also appropriate to the audience plus one level - note that audiences might see you as a little above yourself if you are over-dressed for the occasion or too sloppy, which leaves the impression that you didn't care enough to take the time to dress.

Tailored jackets are a good compromise and can keep those cold chill nerves at bay at the beginning and can be removed when your temperature is back to normal or the heat of the moment takes hold. A jacket can add a more formal note to jeans (where appropriate). Keeping a jacket on can hide nerves (and a tissue in the pocket) but can be uncomfortable if you keep it on for a while. Depending on the occasion and audience, removing the jacket after you have 'settled' might appeal to you. It can also indicate to the audience that you feel comfortable with them.

There is a certain laid-back casual look that self-made millionaires seem to get kudos for - but unless you've changed the world through an incredible innovation I'd think twice before trying it out on your public.

If you are making the Best Man's speech you might find yourself in an ill-fitting suit. Practicing your speech in front of the mirror at home in your underwear might feel comfortable but once in that wretched suit you might lose your nerve.

By the way, you might never again wear that suit or dress assigned to you for the wedding, so if possible have a trial wear. If you are uncomfortable or self-conscious in your fancy, out of your normal style, outfit this will not help reduce the nerves which most likely will accompany the delivery of your carefully planned speech. Wearing it beforehand will give you a chance to assess the risks.

Whenever you can, practice your speech wearing the clothes, or near to the type of clothes you will be wearing on the day.

This brings to mind the first professional speaker I ever hired. It was during the era of the unemployed and I required a specialist speaker to cover the compulsory workplace health and safety component. The speaker duly arrived and delivered, I believe, a reasonable talk on how the workplace has considerable legislation to monitor uncaring employers and protect stupid employees from themselves. Not her words but that was my interpretation. To be honest I really only remember one thing about her presentation - orange. Standing at the back of the room all I could see was noisy orange - hair, dress, shoes, scarf and jangly jewellery- all forming a sunny glow which lit up the room. It was mesmerising, all for the wrong reasons. Having said all that constructive criticism I still remember her.

Over the years of my own wardrobe malfunctions I have opted for low wrinkle, patterned or black dresses which hide a multitude of stains, though I do occasionally have trouble with white stains on black fabric. Vinegar soak before washing does seem to help.

If you are likely to speak regularly you might like to consider your 'look'. Establishing a comfortable and routine sense of self might assist in reducing nerves.

Chapter 16: Be More Of Yourself

How many times have you found yourself doing the opposite of what others told you to do just because you don't want to be told what to do?

It is good to have your own choices—and to make your own decisions. Sometimes, though, it becomes too much—to the point that you no longer see good in what others have advised for you to do. This means that you are suffering from the Reactance Bias.

Resistance is a negative reaction to regulations, rules, and people who are telling you to do something. For example, someone sees you're good in art: you can draw the best interpretations of people, you have a way with colors, etc. However, instead of taking it positively, you begin to feel like people are pushing you to do it, and thus, this thing you actually love doing loses its appeal to you. You then begin to push the idea of drawing away to the extent that you no longer do it, and thus, you choose to do other things that don't really mean much to you. And when that happens, you become mediocre—because you don't try to fulfill your passion.

Reactance happens because of the following:

The feeling that you're now being pressured to do your best, instead of just being able to enjoy the things you love. When you enjoy something, you feel like it's "yours". You don't want to share it to others, and you feel like it belongs to you alone. Now, when other people see how good you are, and say that maybe, you should make a career out of that thing you love, you begin to feel like you're now going to be judged—and you can no longer enjoy it as a whole. Thus, you tend to feel bad about it, and would now see it as a crutch.

Elimination of free behaviors. Before, what you're doing is just a "free behavior", but now, people are saying that maybe, you should try this and that—which makes the free behavior lose its flair. The more important it is to you, the higher the level of reactance because you don't want it to be "taken" away in one way or the other.

Thinking that this is all you can do. And finally, reactance happens when you feel like people would just see you as this artist, this mathematician, etc.--and not as anything else. Hence, you hate being "stereotyped", and would choose to do other things instead.

Learn to Stand Your Ground

It's not easy to feel like you're being pressured—especially when it comes to something you love, and that's why it is understandable that you may react negatively. However, you have to keep in mind that not everyone has the chance to be surrounded by people who'll push them to be the best of who they are, and who would support their passion.

When people tell you that you should make a career out of your passion, or that maybe, you should try this or that, tell them that you appreciate their advice and that you'll think about it. Then, just focus on what you're doing, and see how you can maximize your potential.

Remember: your passion is innate to you—so don't hate it, and don't feel like you should just try to be someone else instead. Be true to yourself—no matter what.

Chapter 17: Vocal Variety

Tori McDermott

Topic: Vocal variety

Learning Objectives: After reviewing the techniques for effective vocal variety, students will be able to:

Demonstrate effective use of vocal variety

Practice and develop full vocal range

Description of Assignment/Activity: This activity is used to get students comfortable with using vocal variety when public speaking. Students will be able to see the effects of poor vocal variety on listeners, as well as work on speaking in front of their peers.

Materials needed:

5-6 Children's Books

White Board

White Board Marker

Prep time: 5 minutes

Assignment time: 15-20 minutes

Instructions for Instructor:

Begin by brainstorming effective vocal variety with your class. What makes an effective speaker and what does not? Effective speakers use vocal variety for emphasis throughout their speeches. Effective speakers have a steady speaking rate and clear projection. Some aspects of a non-effective speaker include, talking too softly, too loudly, sounding monotone throughout the speech, speaking too quickly and speaking too slowly.

After all the responses from the class have been collected, divide the class into groups of four.

Once the class has been divided into groups of four, have the groups pick separate corners of the room and sit in a circle.

Give each group a different children's book. Preferably, pick short books that rhyme. Dr. Seuss books are great for this activity. Most of your students will already know the story and his rhyme scheme is perfect for practicing vocal variety.

Have one student start by asking them to read the book to the rest of the group in a really slow voice. After you have felt like the groups have started getting bored, have the next student in the group read in a new voice. The voices can range from extremely loud to filled with vocal fillers. The object is to have the students demonstrate non-effective vocal variety to each other.

Other ways to speak to demonstrate non-effective vocal variety may include (but are not limited to):

too fast

too slow

too soft

speaking with long pauses

speaking with lots of vocal fillers

speaking too loudly

speaking in a high-pitched voice

speaking in a monotone voice

After each group has gone through all ways of ineffective vocal variety, ask them to brainstorm the characteristics of effective vocal variety.

Tell the groups to employ the characteristics of a effective vocal variety and have the group work together to split up the book to present to the class.

Have each group read their book to the class.

Finish the activity with a brainstorm listing the classes strengths and weaknesses.

Instructions for Students:

Get into groups of four.

One student needs to start us off. I would like you to read the first three pages of the book to your group members in the quietest voice you can.

Now that we have heard the quietest voice, I would like to you pass the book to the person on your right. This student will now read the next three pages as fast as they possibly can. (Continue going around for as long as you like)

Can we brainstorm what was wrong with the ways in which we have been reading the books to each other?

What are some ways in which we could read this book to our groups more effectively?

Each group will work on using these effective vocal variety techniques and in 10 minutes you will present your book to the class as a group.

As a class, what are our strengths with vocal variety? What are our weaknesses?

Necessary Background: This requires a background on the importance of vocal variety and expressiveness within speeches. The students should have some type of knowledge about "Do's" and "Do not's" of effective vocal variety.

Special considerations:

Students may feel uncomfortable reading a children's book in front of their peers. You can always use poetry or song lyrics in place of a children's book.

The students may feel anxious having to read in a silly voice. Preface that this activity is meant to be a fun learning exercise and have the student choose what voice they feel comfortable speaking in.

Debrief: After the first activity, be sure to debrief about the vocal variety that they felt was most effective. Ask your students which way of speaking was the most boring of difficult to listen to. Identify the effective techniques students can use when they are presenting their speeches and the overall importance of using proper vocal variety for maximum audience engagement. These techniques include, but are not limited to emphasizing important parts of the speech through effective vocal variety, have a steady speaking rate, talking loud enough for everyone to hear comfortably and staying away from sounding monotone.

Variations:

Instead of using children's books, you could use poetry or song lyrics.

You can scale this activity up and add more students into the groups to make the groups larger.

Trouble spots:

Make sure to set ground rules for the class about what is appropriate. Make sure all students know that this is supposed to be a fun activity and that no students should feel embarrassed during this activity. This activity is fun and may cause students to get off track, make sure to keep students focused and constantly busy.

Make sure to warn nearby teachers if you plan on having your students get loud.

Chapter 18: Making The Most Of Employment Interviews

One of the most important opportunities you will ever have to speak publicly may be in an interview for a job. The market for many employment opportunities is very competitive. It is imperative that your oral communication skills are tuned to be the best that they can possibly be, and that, of course, takes preparation and practice.

Here are tips for preparing for an interview:

The first thing you must do is to find out as much as you can about the company for which you are interviewing. Often, this is not that difficult due to the wonders of technology. Today, most companies have a web presence. Be sure and visit the company's website and look at their history and the products and services that they market, and then try and get a sense of the company culture. Then, visit a couple of websites that focus on providing profiles of companies, such as www.glassdoors.com and www.linkedin.com. Glassdoors is an excellent source because the site invites employees of companies to submit reviews that focus on the quality of the work environment. In addition, some of these sites even offer possible interview questions that companies may use to assess candidates.

Once you have gathered your research, sit down and prepare a response to the following two questions:

Can you please tell us a little bit about yourself?

This is what is known as an open-ended question, which means that it cannot be adequately answered by a "yes" or a "no." Keep in mind that your answer to this question, and everything else you say during the interview, should be designed to gain further consideration for the position for which you are interviewing. Keep your response focused on those qualities you possess that will make you an asset to the company. DO NOT discuss your love of roller skating, for example, unless of course you are interviewing for a spot on a local roller derby team.

Shape your response in the form of a story, if you can. Perhaps you can speak chronologically about your work experience that highlights skills in which your potential employer may be interested. Or, you can highlight successes you have achieved in your educational and occupational history that relate to the job for which you are applying. After you speak about yourself in a very positive way, conclude your response by stating your strong interest in the position and then offer reasons why the position interests you.

Why should we hire you above any other candidate?

You will notice that this question is also an open-ended one. The reason employers ask open-ended questions is that they want to hear you speak, and you can bet that they are watching your body language as much as they are listening to your answer as you respond to the question (If you have not yet read it, make sure that you read Chapter 3 in this book, which discusses the importance of monitoring and perfecting your nonverbal communication).

This question, and similar questions, are invitations for you to persuade the interviewer (or interviewers) to hire you. If you have done your homework by effectively researching the company and by getting a sense of what they are looking for in an employee, you should be well-prepared for your task. Make sure that you have prepared three reasons they should consider you above other candidates. The reasons you give should directly reflect upon your ability to be an asset to the position for which they are hiring, as well as for the company.

It is strongly recommended that you practice your answers to these two questions in front of your webcam so that you can play the recordings back and critique them. It's even better if you can solicit a trusted friend or colleague to evaluate them as well. Remember the importance of eye contact, a strong voice, and assertive body language as you record your responses to these and any other questions you think you may be asked.

Always be sure to prepare at least five questions you can ask your interviewers when they ask you if you have any that you would like to discuss. Your questions should be relevant to the company and to the position, and the research you conduct on the company during your preparation for the interview should be a great resource for you to get some ideas about what sort of questions you should ask. Another great source you can use to get some ideas about possible questions is the job description that lists the position.

There are two major reasons to prepare questions as you prepare for an employment interview:

Asking questions allows you to gain a broader perspective regarding the company and the position. Obviously, the more that you know about where you will be working and what you will be doing, the better able you will be decide whether to accept an employment offer if one is made.

Asking questions of potential employers sends a strong message to them that you have done some research and some thinking about the company and the position before the interview. **Those who conduct employment interviews expect interviewees to ask questions and they often judge candidates on what sort of questions they ask.**

What sort of questions should you ask in an employment interview? It's best to keep your questions focused on the company and the position. Here are a few suggestions:

"Are there any additional expectations you will require of me that we have not

discussed if I am hired for this position?"
This question may yield additional information regarding the position that had not been previously discussed.

"Can you describe a typical day for someone holding the position for which you are interviewing?" A question like this has the potential to increase your education about just what it is that you will be doing if you are offered the position.

"What is the training process for the position? Who will train me? Will I be trained individually or in a group? Where does the training take place and who does the training?" Questions regarding training are important because you want to make sure that you will have the knowledge and the skill set necessary to do the job in a way that meets the company's expectations. If they plan on hiring you knowing that you do not yet possess that skill set or knowledge base, it's good to know up front how they plan on making sure you are prepared to execute the duties of the position.

"What are your performance expectations for the person you hire in this role? "Will those expectations change over time?" "How often will I be reviewed for performance and what does that process look like?" It's important for a candidate to have a good understanding of job expectations and how performance will be assessed. Asking these questions will yield information for the candidate and send a message to the interviewer that the candidate has an interest in meeting or exceeding expectations.

"Can you tell me a bit about the company's goals and where it hopes to be in five years?" This question allows the candidate to make a judgement about whether he or she has an opportunity for growth within the company.

"What are the opportunities for advancement in the company for people who hold this position?" This is a more direct way of yielding information about potential employment paths within the company.

"What happens next in the interview process?" This is a natural question that should always be asked if the interviewers do not take the time to describe the next steps of the interview process to you.

"Have I adequately answered your questions regarding my qualifications for this position? Is there any other information that you need from me?" **This is a great question because it allows the candidate to make sure that all bases have been covered during the interview.**

Employment interviews require excellent public speaking skills related to both the informational and the persuasive categories. Employers invite people into their domains to ascertain the appropriateness of those candidates for employment. Those candidates who are able to effectively communicate how their education, experience, and skill sets qualify them as the best choices for positions will usually get the jobs. Do your research, organize your resume, anticipate questions, prepare great answers to those questions, and prepare intelligent and thoughtful questions for your interviewers. Practicing these tips will make you stand out in your quest for quality employment.

Questions to Ponder:

What are your successes and achievements that may help potential employers view you as a great candidate for employment?

How can you research a company for which you would like to work besides visiting their website?

Chapter 19: Index Of Easy Sermon Styles:

Verse-by-Verse Bible Study- Explained:

Verse-by-verse Bible study is as simple as it sounds. It is the process of taking a passage of scripture and going through each verse. This is for a Bible Study setting where everyone is sitting in a circle or able to easily talk and research together each verse. Some tools you could use: Cross-referencing, looking up words in the dictionary, using a thesaurus, using different versions or translations of the Bible.

3 Points – Explained:

Using a point-illustrated system can be a helpful way to teach and also provide an easy way for people to learn. There are three objectives that are involved in this style of sermon.

First by reading through the Scripture Passage and finding good points that explain the passage.

162

Second, cross-referencing each point you have and explain clearly what it means.

Lastly, application: to figure out a way that you can easily make each point into a practical thing that people can do to respond to the Scripture.

Lecture – Explained:

A lecture is more of a 'controlled ramble' where you are reading through the facts of something and leaving little to no room for personal opinion.

Bible Story – Explained:

A Bible Story style of preaching is very effective when trying to get an audience to learn one specific objective. The Bible is full of stories and parables that each drives home their own message. Some don't need explaining and others have explanations. Bible Stories can be used to teach and explain the bible very easily. They leave a lot of room for people to interact with and apply the truths in the story to their own life. You can attach Bible stories to every kind of sermon style

163

and you can also use then independently as a quick sermon on the go. (Great for sharing)

Testimony – Explained:

Giving your testimony and sharing your life story are very different but often get confused as the same thing. A testimony addresses three things. First, what was your driving force in life before accepting Jesus in your heart? Second, how did you find Jesus? And lastly, what is your life like now? A testimony needs to stick to a structure when sharing with people. I.e. this is what life was like before, and this is what life is like now. The overall message needs to point to past present and future.

Life Story – Explained:

Sharing your life story and giving your testimony are very different but often get confused as the same thing. Sharing your life story is talking about your life. Focusing of things you have journeyed through without Jesus or with Him. There isn't really a transition or structure to follow from darkness to light when you are sharing your life story. The overall message needs to point to Jesus in your life now.

Bonus Material and Notes from: How to Lead a Devotional

Know your audience. When picking your topic and props it is important to know the age group you are talking to. You need to know what you're going to be walking into. Is it for Children? Is it for youth? Young adults? Adults? Seniors? Single moms? Knowing this information can help you prepare a better devotion.

Know what your talking about, but don't be a know it all. There is a fine line between knowing what you are talking about and coming across as someone that doesn't care about feedback from the group.

Always start with Prayer. God always has a calming effect when we start with prayer. If you are nervous or anxious you will quickly notice that your nerves will settle if you start with praying. It does not need to be a lengthily prayer. Something simple is fine. 'Thank you Jesus for today and this opportunity that You've given me to share. Please help me talk about the things that You have helped prepare in my heart. In Jesus Name Amen.'

Pick one topic. Keep in mind that you are sharing a devotional and not preaching a sermon. You want to be insightful and give time for people to respond.

Share from one scripture or one scripture passage. The main thing is to keep what you are talking about as simple as possible. Try not to read passages from scripture that are longer then 2-3 verses. And try not to jump from one verse to the next, back and forth in your bible. If you can find one verse that says everything you need said, then just stick with that one verse.

Talk about you. Share a personal story or an example from your life that relates to what you are talking about.

Using props. A younger audience will respond better to a craft as your prop. Youth or young adults may respond well to a short video chip. An older audience may respond better to a passage out of a book as your prop. There are so many different things you could use as props. It is important to know your audience. However, if your props are going to be a distraction then don't use them.

Conclusion/audience application. (Set a time limit) This is where you engage the audience. You can write up some discussion questions and ask the audience. Of you can pair people up and get them to ask each other the questions. You can make a handout that they can read more scriptures about the topic on their own time.

Always end with Prayer. It is easy to bring everyone back together to pray. Again, try not to be long winded. Try to keep it simple. Jesus, thank you for what we have learnt today. Please help us to apply your scripture to our lives. Amen.'

Thank you for taking the time to read through this lesson. My prayer is that you will learn new ways to share the gospel. To be prepared to talk about your faith in Jesus, in season and out of season.

Chapter 20: Body Language

Body language can be expressed in many different ways that can effectively enhance the quality of your speech. The purpose of body language is to direct the audience's focus towards you while you are speaking. In other words, it is used to strengthen the words that you are saying because you are now communicating yourself to the audience in two ways instead of just one, where you are speaking.

I'm not going to tell you what you kinds of movements or hand motions you should specifically concentrate on, because different people will feel comfortable with different kinds of body language. What I will say, however, is that generally speaking, the more body language you express during your speech, the better your overall speech will be. It is never a bad idea to use plenty of body language, but there should be moments in your speech where you should keep your movements to a minimum to diversify your performance. This will prevent your audience from getting bored too easily. Also, don't use too much body language, as this might seem a little hokey. The audience will be able to pick up on this. Usually, this is not a problem for most speakers. When was the last time you've ever attended a speech where you thought the speaker used "too much" body language? Probably never. If you are in doubt about whether or not you are using too much body language in your speeches, start off with using whatever you consider as "less than a normal" amount of body language.

Another thing that I will mention is that you should vary the speed of your body language, such as the movement of your hands to emphasize a point, throughout the speech.

Here's an intermediate level tip that I would suggest you should use in your speeches. If you are using hand movements while you are talking about a very valid point, such as stating some sort of a fact to an audience, slow down the pace of your hand movements as you say the sentence that include that fact. For example, you should slow yourself down so that the audience can really concentrate on your words when you say, "Did you know that, **seventy percent of Americans are overweight**?" The italicized part of that sentence is when you should slow down body language by at least a little. On the other hand, when you wish to talk about a personal opinion, you should try speeding up the part of the sentence where you state your opinion. For example, when you say, "Kids these days are **stupid**," try speeding your body language up when you say the italicized word in that sentence. It'll make people focus on that word because they way you said it sticks out from the way you've been speaking from the rest of the sentence.

Of course, you could do the opposite of what I've been saying, and the technique will probably still work. There is no "correct" way of public speaking.

Is Public Speaking a Skill or Is It a Talent?

It is both, just like almost anything in life.

Have you ever participated in some sort of activity in which you were undeniably better than everyone else for some unknown reason? The unknown reason is that you had talent in that area. Public speaking is just like any other form of art or science in that talent is a factor that determines your performance beforehand. The practice you do to hone your skill is just that - a way of honing your skill so that you improve. If you have to ask yourself if you are a natural at public speaking, then chances are that you are not. If you were, you would know within the first or second speech you've ever given. If you've ever looked at a hundred-person audience, and wished it were a million-person audience, then you probably are a natural. If you aren't a natural, then it's not a big deal because it just means that there is something else you are very good at. Everyone is good in at least one thing.

No matter what your level of talent in public speaking is, it is important to practice your skill, and not become so arrogant to the point where you think you know it all. Bad things tend to happen when you take your talents for granted. Allow me to illustrate. Let's say that Roger Federer, who is obviously a very gifted tennis player, never practiced any more tennis starting today. Do you think his chances of winning more trophies will decrease substantially? Likewise, if you took the worst tennis player you've ever seen in your life, and made him train 8 hours a day, would you put your money on him or her winning any tournaments in the future?

Lastly, body posture is an overrated element to try to control for a speech. While it is good to vary your body posture throughout a speech if you can, some people are not able to do this due to age or other health reasons. In fact, having poor body posture can be a good thing to have because it will make the audience pay more attention to you. The downside is that if you have poor body posture AND you give a terrible speech, the audience will tend to dismiss your words and their thoughts will wander.

This doesn't matter though, because this is not an integral part of public speaking that makes or breaks a speech. Think about it this way. Do you choose your friends based on how they act and behave and what they say, or do you judge them based on their posture?

Speech Fatigue

Another thing that I'm willing to bet that most public speaking books do not talk about is something I like to call "speech fatigue". Speech fatigue is basically how a speaker starts to get tired of speaking if he or she is required to speak for as long as fifteen to forty-five minutes, or even more at a time. However, chances are, that if you are required to give a speech for at least an hour, then you are probably getting paid a lot for the speech because you are good at public speaking. Even then, if that is true, then you still might be able to learn something from this short lesson.

Speech fatigue is natural, and is no different than how a physically untrained person feels exhausted as they attempt to run a mile. Speech fatigue can begin to affect a speaker in as little as four to five minutes after they begin their speech, and after about ten to fifteen minutes, they will really start to feel it. Their mouths may start to feel dry, and they might even start to feel their performance getting to be a little predictable.

So how do you deal with speech fatigue? The only one way that I really know of is to simply rehearse the speech (starting days before the actual date of the actual speech) at least a dozen times from beginning to end. You can do this in front of a mirror or in front of a wall, or even in front of nothing. Rehearsing your speech many times will help you build the stamina required for a long speech. If your speech is meant to be about an hour long, then please practice for at least twelve hours. If your speech is thirty minutes long, then please practice for at least six hours, and so forth.

One thing I would like for you to remember about speech fatigue is that usually, the audience will be able to detect it in you if you really do start to feel tired, but this is not a bad thing at all. If you have been giving an excellent or even average presentation all along, the audience will almost always seem willing to continue listening to you, and not mind your fading energy at all. They will understand. In fact, they will take it as a sign of honesty, and like you even more usually. If you were a gym teacher in school, should you be frustrated with the students that don't seem to be athletic enough to participate in most of the activities? Of course not. The same applies with public speaking.

On the other hand, if you've been giving a terrible speech the whole time, then the audience will be glad to detect speech fatigue within you. They will interpret your tiredness as a sign that the speech is probably about to end, and they will look forward to you leaving the stage. Either way, speech fatigue is a win-win situation, unless the audience paid money to listen to you. In that case, speech fatigue is bad, but if you are getting paid to speak, you should be sensible enough to know that you are responsible for rehearsing a lot before a performance.

Conclusion

Congratulations, you have made it to the conclusion of this book. The reason why I say congratulations is because 70% of most people who buy books never read the book past the first chapter. Either this book was way too good or way too short. LOL a little "vision humor" for you. I wanted to make this book simple and to the point to get you started on your path as a speaker. I don't believe in having too much fluff, so I made sure to give you exactly what you need to become a success.

There are a few things I want you to keep in mind. While this book will help you to get started, if you are serious about your speaking career, I most definitely believe that taking things a step further is vital. There is so much to developing your talk and getting booked.

In fact, one of the things I teach in my Speaking for Profits Course with S.Y.S.T.E.M. Mastery University is that there are actually up to 20 different types of legs that you can use in your talk. I go over all of those 20 legs for you. I even show you how to go deeper into your introduction so that it truly engages the audience and has them ready to buy from you before you ever make an offer.

Being a great speaker does take work and being willing to develop your skill. For me, it has taken more than 10 years to develop this skill. On public speaking courses and coaching alone, I've spent more than $9,000 in the past four years. When I to combine that with personal development, I've spent more than $100,000 in the past 5 years.

I encourage you to further your education and become all the way qualified in your speaking. If you are not able to take that further step, at least get started. I see so many visionaries that have so much in them, and they are waiting on the perfect moment to do their first event. I can tell you that there is never a perfect time. So stop using that as an excuse. Go out there and find yourself a location, post your event on Eventbrite.com, Meetup.com, and Facebook.com, and get to promoting.

Will you mess up on your first event? Possibly, but don't let that keep you from taking action. My first event, I had no clue what I was doing, but I know that if I hadn't made a decision to do that first small event of 10 people, I wouldn't be living the dream today! Let nothing stop you! Let no one stop you! You have what it takes, so go out and impact the world!

Make sure to visit my website Bonus.SpeakingForProfits.com to get resources, tools and more! If you want to know more about being one of my students in S.Y.S.T.E.M. Mastery, you can also schedule a

"Vision Strategy Session" with one of my Vision Team members. Also, if you enjoyed this book please refer someone to the website to purchase it, and don't forget to leave a review for me on Amazon! If you leave a review, I will send you a free gift on my latest Ebook! Just make sure to include your email on your review. I appreciate you, and I pray that you are impacted and inspired to take action!

CPSIA information can be obtained
at www.ICGtesting.com
Printed in the USA
BVHW040955220720
584330BV00009B/286

9 781989 990070